Angel in the Kitchen

❧⚭

Wit & Wisdom Inspired by Food, Cooking, Kitchen Tools and Appliances!

Books by Tom & Wilma English
available from DEAD LETTER PRESS:

ANGEL IN THE KITCHEN 2: A SECOND SERVING OF WIT & WISDOM
INSPIRED BY FOOD, COOKING, KITCHEN TOOLS AND APPLIANCES
(186 pages • ISBN: 9780996693608)

DIET FOR DREAMERS: INSPIRATION TO FEED YOUR DREAMS,
ENCOURAGEMENT TO FOSTER YOUR CREATIVITY!
(162 pages • ISBN: 9780979633577)

THE HEART OF AN ANGEL: BECOMING GOD'S MESSENGERS
OF LOVE AND HOSPITALITY TO A WORLD IN NEED
(202 pages • ISBN: 9780996693615)

SPIRITUAL BOOT CAMP FOR CREATORS & DREAMERS:
ENCOURAGEMENT, INSPIRATION AND BASIC TRAINING TO HELP YOU
ACHIEVE YOUR DREAMS   (272 pages • ISBN: 9780996693691)

Angel in the Kitchen

❧ ❦

Wit & Wisdom Inspired by Food, Cooking, Kitchen Tools and Appliances!

Wilma Espaillat English
And Tom English

DEAD LETTER PRESS
BOX 134, NEW KENT, VA 23124-0134

Angel in the Kitchen
First published 2015 by Ravens' Reads
An imprint of
DEAD LETTER PRESS

This edition © February 2023

The articles collected in *Angel in the Kitchen* originally appeared on the website www.AngelattheDoor.com and were slightly revised for this book.

Printed in the United States of America

**ISBN-10: 0-9966936-0-2
ISBN-13: 978-0-9966936-0-8**

DEAD LETTER PRESS
BOX 134, NEW KENT, VIRGINIA 23124-0134

CONTENTS:

Angels in the Kitchen!

...Since the creation of the world [God's] invisible attributes, His eternal power and divine nature, have been clearly seen, being understood through what has been made....
—Romans 1:20 NASB

...These words are faithful and true; and the Lord God of the holy prophets has sent His angel to show...the things which are necessary that they be done quickly.
—Revelation 22:6 Jubilee Bible 2000

At the beginning of 2015 we launched AngelAtTheDoor.com, a website featuring three ongoing series of internet articles. The best articles from two of these series, *Diet for Dreamers* and *Encouragement for Creators*, were collected in book form as *Diet for Dreamers: Inspiration to Feed Your Dreams, Encouragement to Foster Your Creativity*.

Our third series of articles is called *Angel in the Kitchen: Wit and Wisdom Inspired by Food, Cooking, Kitchen Tools and Appliances*, which continues to appear weekly on our website. Our goal for *Angel in the Kitchen* was to share nuggets of wisdom and truths about life, love, and relationships, as well as the nature and character of the God of the Bible—*the God of Abraham, Isaac, and Israel*; and we hoped to accomplish this in a unique, entertaining, and creative way.

For fresh ideas and a seemingly endless source of

inspiration we needed to look no further than the hundreds of food items, gadgets, utensils, and equipment that fill the typical household kitchen (the "heart" of the home). As we worked with these familiar everday items, for cooking, cleaning, and serving the numerous guests who often drop by to visit, we realized that each had a special message to impart.

We found that many cooking techniques, such as simmering and microwaving; both natural and processed foods, such as eggs and onions, canned goods and boxed items; and many of the common sights and practices found daily in our kitchen, were analogous to an incredible wealth of Biblical insights. Suddenly, the blender was begging to share its story, the crock-pot was crying out to be heard, and the toaster wouldn't stop talking. Every *thing*—actually, every *one!*—has a special, anointed message to deliver to our readers.

In the Bible, God has an army of "heavenly messengers" called *angels*. Sometimes these supernatural beings visit earth in the guise of travelers on the byways of life. But in a manner of speaking, *anything* God uses to speak to us, becomes His "messenger." In this sense, God's "angels" can visit us in a variety of forms.

We can acquire truth from the Bible, as well as from pastors and priests, rabbis and missionaries; and even from music, television and movies. But we can also hear God speak to us in the roar of the ocean surf, see His wisdom in a blade of grass, and learn important lessons from industrious ants and puffy rain clouds. If we're attuned to what God is trying to teach us, we quickly realize that every creation in nature, including the people in our lives, and really, every thing in life itself, has a special message to impart— an *angelic* role to play.

Over the past several months we've introduced our internet readers to all the "angels" in our kitchen: those appliances, gadgets and food items which continue to teach us lessons about our often crazy adventures here on planet earth. We wrote, among many other things, about our twin microwave ovens, Luke and Nuke; about the call of the Keurig; and how Fridgey (our refrigerator) enjoys the nightlife. We've discussed God and groceries; culinary oddballs and weird cookbooks; the spiritual significance of Tupperware; and what happens when "The Cheese Stands Alone"—and we've had a blast doing it! No one is as creative as our Lord, the Master Chef!

Sixty-six of the best articles from *Angel in the Kitchen* are collected here for your enjoyment. We hope these "kitchen angels" will make you laugh, cry and think. We're confident that upon finishing this inspiring and encouraging collection you, too, will believe a toaster can talk!

Wilma Espaillat English
Tom English
New Kent, VA

Pets and appliances on a mission. Walt Disney's 1963 adventure film *The Incredible Journey* (based on a 1961 novel by Sheila Burnford); and (below) Walt Disney's 1987 animated feature *The Brave Little Toaster* (based on the award-winning 1980 novella by Thomas M. Disch, who called the tale a "bedtime story for small appliances").

Our Toaster Talks!

A toaster can talk? *No!* Of course not! Well ... actually ... in a manner of speaking. *Ahem*, please just read on.

Our house seemingly lies still at night, but all is not at rest. Down in the kitchen it's easy to imagine a party is in full swing. The clock on the range occasionally flashes and keeps time to the whispers, winks and furtive glances made by our appliances. No, we haven't lost our minds. Although we may have overactive imaginations. Sometimes we just get inspired.

There's an old Disney movie we enjoy, about a gang of appliances left behind in a summer cottage. When these anthropomorphic gadgets realize they've been long forgotten, they set out to find their master. Think Disney's *The Incredible Journey*, only instead of two dogs and a Siamese cat, this time our heroes are a loudmouthed radio, a whiny electric blanket, a fairly "bright" desk lamp, a tough vacuum cleaner (named Kirby); and their intrepid leader, the eponymous hero of *The Brave Little Toaster*!

Before we knew it, we were naming all our appliances! We have a large antique-style radio we dubbed Orson, in honor of the contributions made to the early medium by Mr. Welles, the famed writer, director, and star of "the broadcast that shocked America," *The War of the Worlds*); the kitchen range is "Sparky" (when we switch on one of his gas burners, he snaps at us and sparks to life); "Luke" and "Nuke" (twin microwave ovens that allow us to cook two frozen dinners at the same time!); and then there's "Fridgey."

We live in the woods, in a house we named Woodhaven, and we love the peace and quiet. Outside, our days amid the trees are filled only with the sounds of birds, our nights punctuated by the lonely calls of a whippoorwill. Inside, things are just a bit more lively: our computer hums softly to himself (That's Hal; do you remember *2001: A Space Odyssey*?); the printer (Flash) clicks and whirs; all to the accompaniment of the ticking, murmuring, gurgling and, sometimes, even groaning sounds of the appliances. All these sounds become far more noticeable at night. That's usually the time when a house really starts to talk.

When we first got our new refrigerator, before we got used to what he wanted to tell us, we'd often awaken from a deep sleep, thinking someone was downstairs raiding the kitchen: Fridgey calls out to us like a distant foghorn shrouded in the night mist, gently reassuring us that he's protecting our food from spoiling. Periodically he alerts us that there's plenty of ice ahead (cubes, not bergs) for a glass of tea or soda, by periodically sounding off with an encouraging *ker-chunk!* Now, whenever we hear Fridgey talking in the middle of night, we just go back to sleep. We've come to recognize the sound of his voice!

Apart from learning just how silly we can be, you can glean another lesson from this story. Each day our appliances let us know exactly "what they're about" as they go through their routines. All of our kitchen friends have discovered their voice! We all need to do the same.

Most of us have heard that writers are frequently admonished to "find your own voice." Until they do, they tend to imitate the style of some other writer. Then, one day, everything finally seems to click, and a writer discovers his or her own unique voice! But we all need to find our voice, not just writers. That's what makes life so wonderful: we're not trying to be you, you're not trying to be her, etc. When we sing, we each have our own key! We know who we are and what we're about. We each discover our own, God-given voice.

Apple co-founder Steve Jobs once said, "Your time is limited, so don't waste it living someone else's life. ...Don't let the noise of others' opinions drown out your own inner voice. And most important, have the courage to follow your heart and intuition."

Thank You [God] for making (each of us) so wonderfully complex! Your workmanship is marvelous! —Psalm 139:14 NLT

The Call of the Keurig

In the 1983 movie *Mr. Mom*, Michael Keaton (aka Batman aka Birdman) plays an out-of-work engineer who agrees to stay home and take care of the house and kids so that his wife (played by Teri Garr) can return to her old ad agency job and support the family. (Well, when the movie premiered the idea seemed a little more radical than it does now.) In a memorable scene, Keaton's character, Jack, asks the kids where mommy keeps the vacuum.

The kids respond, "You mean Mister Jaws?" Jack laughs at the idea of giving a household appliance a name, especially a name like Mister Jaws; but that's before he's had a chance to witness the monster in action!

Last year we bought a new Shark vacuum. Today, after a period of adjustment, we can honestly state that we absolutely adore our ferocious little *Sharky*! No, no, *Shark* is actually the name of the company. Ironically, the word perfectly suits this powerful vacuum's aggressive personality. Once, we allowed him to get a little too close to the drapes, and he ended up eating a good two feet of the fabric before we managed to pry them from his hungry jaws! So, yeah, appliances can have, or at least seem to have, their own personalities—like our Keurig coffeemaker.

We love our Keurig. We often wonder how we ever managed without him. And wouldn't you know it, we sometimes think that he wonders the same thing! Okay, so he's got a little bit of an ego, but maybe he's got good reason to be proud. After all, Keurig feels he's the best at what he does. In no time flat, he can brew a perfect cup of coffee. But wait! Not only does he conjure up a perfect java while you watch, but he also invites audience participation! As he performs, narrating every step of the process, he sends us these cute little glowing messages, such as "Select your serving size" or "Ready to brew"!

But Keurig is very vocal, too! As he works, he gives off these audible sighs of contentment; and after his work is done, Keurig gurgles and hisses to let us know that "Coffee's ready!"

I gotta tell ya, I just love what I do!

What's he really saying? We like to think that Keurig is telling us that he truly enjoys what he's doing and that he loves to serve; that the little guy's message in this hectic, often aggravating world is, "Hey, life can be tough, so how about a latte?"

Whether we realize it or not, we all have a message, a story to tell, something we need to share.

What's your message? What do you daily tell the world? We sincerely hope it's a message of love!

I may be able to speak the languages of men and even of angels, but if I do not have love, it will sound like noisy brass.
—1 Corinthians 13:1 NLV

Mack the Knife

The knife block on our kitchen counter does a great job keeping the many different types of cutlery we need, in a neat and organized fashion. One day we emptied the block in order to sharpen all our knives. Well, getting all those blades back into their proper slots was a bit of a challenge. There's a long, bread knife, a butcher knife, a cheese knife, a carving knife, a filleting knife, steak knives, a menacing looking cleaver, and something called a rocking chopper!

Some have serrated edges, some have straight; some are pointed, some not so; there are wide blades, short blades; rounded tips, slanted tips; knives for peeling, carving, slicing, dicing...wow, we sure hope Norman Bates isn't reading this! (Yes, today we're acting like a couple of cut-ups! *Groan!*)

Each of these kitchen tools serves a specific function. Each is highly useful. Unfortunately, each is also designed to perfectly fit into its very own designated slot. We spent several

minutes trying to remember what went where, and ended up trying out various slots for various knives. We finally got everything back in place, but this got us to thinking (which, for us, is always a dangerous thing).

People are like knives! Yes, at times, some of us can be very cutting, but that's not our thought for today; we are all different, and we all have

9

something we're particularly good at, something we were specially designed for and called to do in life. Because of this, each of us fits into the world in a unique way. We each have our own place in the grand scheme of things...our own—wait for it!—slot to fill.

Are you in your proper slot? Are you doing what you're called to do? Are you in the right place at the right time? In your job, are doing what you were created to do? At school or college, are you really trying hard to see where you fit? And why? And how? Are you traveling the right road in order to find where you belong?

Tough questions, we know; and sometimes we realize we're really not where we should be. What do you think? Do you need to change your focus or your goals? Maybe you need to take some night courses to broaden your horizons, change your major, or develop that neglected talent. Is it too late to

find your proper slot in life? Are you kidding? It's never too late to realize and settle into the place where God wants you.

Of course, there's always the chance you've found a slot that fits. Is it the perfect fit? The one uniquely designed and designated for you by God? Maybe, just maybe, you've even found *several* slots that sort of fit. However, only one is the *perfect* fit, and if you're jumping from slot to slot, you're undoubtedly keeping some other sharp person from finding his or her own unique and perfect niche in life.

Are you trying to be the proverbial "Jack (or Mack) of all trades—but master of none"! Focus, friends. Find the right fit, and then be satisfied with your slot. "The steps of a [good] man are directed and established by the Lord when He delights in his way [and He busies Himself with his every step]." (Psalm 37:23 Amplified Bible)

Know What You're Cut Out For

"A place for everything, and everything in its place." That's the key to being organized, but it's also the key to unity and harmony within any type of community or family. Everyone one of us has a special place in this world, a special calling, talent, role to play.

Previously we stated that people are like knives in a knife block. We're all pretty sharp at something, but we were each uniquely designed to perform one or two special func-tions extremely well; and we all need to work at fitting in: we need to find our slot.

Imagine trying to cut your steak with a cheese knife. Good luck with that. Or imagine peeling a potato with a butcher knife. Goodbye, fingers. We all know we need to select the right tool for the right job, *right?* But have any of you ever tried to use a butter knife to pry the lid from a paint can, or to tighten the screws on something? Wouldn't it be easier (and safer) to grab the right tool?

Sometimes, we know exactly which knife we need for a job, go to reach for it, and...it's not where it's supposed to be. So we either stop cooking long enough to locate it, or improvise and use a different knife. Some-times, after improvising, we also need to find a Band-Aid. That's why a kitchen runs so much more smoothly when we understand the purpose of each specialized piece of cutlery, and we keep each piece properly positioned in the right slot of the knife block.

Apply this to work, church, family, or any organization. Organizations need to be ... *ahem*, organized. Especially families. Within a group, the members need to know who's good at what, and then assign each task to the person best capable of doing it. And that person should be available when needed.

Families run smoother when there's a fair and logical division of labor: everyone has a job, everyone knows whose job is what, and everyone is playing his or her part. Dads have a slot that moms will find hard to fill, and vice-versa. In church, teachers shouldn't be playing the organ, greeters shouldn't be handling the finances, and pastors don't have time to type up the bulletin.

Folks, *specializing* is not a dirty word. It allows the most efficient use of time and talent, keeps things orderly and running smoothly, and enables everyone to play a part and discover their gifting. Would you want a podiatrist examining your eyes? Of course not. So, find the slot where you best fit, and be there when you're needed. Maintain your "family" group the way you would your knife block: a place (role/task/function) for everyone, and everyone in his or her proper slot.

One last thought: "...God is not the author of confusion, but of peace...." (1 Corinthians 14:33 KJB) So then: "...Be sure that everything is done properly and in order." (1 Corinthians 14:40 NLT)

After all, if you haphazardly toss all your knives into a kitchen drawer, the resulting jumble of blades is not a good situation, at all. When you need a specific knife for a task, you'll waste a good deal of time sorting through the chaos, and you may even slice a knuckle or two.

Meanwhile, the knives themselves will probably start rubbing each other the wrong way. A few will grow dull. Some may even get bent out of shape. Just saying.

The Mighty Thor!

A hero is born! Onward, dear reader:

We love making smoothies—a splash of skim milk and a cup of frozen strawberries and blackberries. (The blackberries grow wild in the woods behind our home.) And sometimes we toss a scoop of protein powder into our smoothies. But we encountered a big problem while making our favorite shake. Our first blender is too mild-mannered to accomplish the task of grinding and mixing the icy fruit and other ingredients. Actually, we're being kind: it's downright wimpy! It grumbled at us every time it had to make a smoothie. Its motor even whined!

So we retired *Wimpy* to the garage, with the promise we'd bring it out once in a while, for easier jobs, like blending a chocolate malt. Then we put in a call for help, and Thor arrived—via UPS—to save the day!

Thor is a rather impressive, even imposing, blender. It pulverizes frozen strawberries and other fruits. When it whirls its hammer—*uh*, blades—it creates a whirlpool of delicious smoothie! Until....

One day—*gasp!*—Thor stopped working! He'd been fine the previous morning, but when we pulled him out of the appliance garage (Thor prefers calling it *Avengers Tower*), tossed in some fruit, and punched the button.... *Nothing!*

No action. No hearty battle cry. *Nothing.*

"Thor," we lamented, "Call down the lightning and make our smoothie!" *Nothing.*

Fear not! Thor is alive and well; and whipping smoothies into delicious submission. But on that particular morning, when we pulled him from the appliance garage, we accidentally unplugged his power cord. *Doh!* Thor couldn't get the job done because he was no longer connected to the power source. Once he was plugged back in, he was again able to call down the thunder and rescue us from ... *uh* ... being hungry!

Lesson learned: You can have the world's mightiest kitchen appliances, but if they're not plugged in to the source of power, they'll never do the jobs they were created for. *Betcha* know what's coming next.

God created each of us for a special purpose. We each have great value and a particular set of talents and abilities bestowed upon us by our Heavenly Father. And part of the joy of life is discovering His purpose and plan for each of us. But it's no great mystery.

We were created in His image and set upon earth to make a positive contribution: specifically, to help those around us—especially, to point the way to salvation through Christ—and to bring glory to God. In other words, we were designed to reflect God's character to the world. "...let your light shine before others, that they may see your good deeds and glorify your Father in heaven." (Matthew 5:16 NIV)

But we need to be plugged in! If we're going to "call down the lightning"; if we're going to tap into God's Holy Spirit power and anointing (His divine, supernatural influence which is necessary to accomplish His will and impact the world for His eternal purposes), then we need to maintain an unbroken connection to *The Power!*

First, we do our utmost NOT to impede the flow of current. Sin separates us from God. So, when we fail, we must run to Him, confess our weaknesses, and ask Him to cleanse us— of anything that could drive a wedge in the relationship we each have with the God of the Universe. Sin, by the way, is not just a list of DON'Ts. Sin is *anything* that separates YOU from God. "...If we confess our sins to him, he is faithful and just to forgive us... and to cleanse us from all wickedness." (1 John 1:9 NLT)

Second, we never cut the lines of communication. To the contrary, we must remain vigilant over everything we do. We must stay in constant touch with our Lord, through daily prayer and Bible reading.

Prayer is a fancy word for talking to our Lord: sharing your thoughts, your concerns, your problems; telling Him how much you appreciate the things He's accomplished for you (including salvation); and reminding Him (and yourself) exactly how exceedingly perfect and wonderful He is! "If you abide in me, and my words abide in you, ask whatever you wish, and it will be done for you." (John 15:7 ESV)

Third, we need to stay in fellowship with other believers, encouraging and strengthening one another. There's great strength in numbers, folks. "Let us think of ways to motivate one another to acts of love and good works. And let us not neglect our meeting together...but encourage one another, especially now that the day of his return is drawing near." (Hebrews 10:24-25 NLT)

By the way, who's the *true* God of Thunder? None other than the God of Abraham, Isaac and Israel! "Listen carefully to the thunder of God's voice.... It rolls across the heavens, and his lightning flashes in every direction." (Job 37:2-3 NLT)

The Faithfully Fueled Flames of Sparky!

We'd like to share a little more about *Sparky*, our gas range! (Yes, we can be silly at times! What's your excuse?) Sparky is faithful; even in the midst of a pro-longed power outage, our trustworthy kitchen friend didn't let us down! Please read on.

One fateful Christmas Eve, over a decade ago, Virginia and several surrounding states endured a massive ice storm. The day before, we had prepared a variety of tempting treats to enjoy throughout the holidays, including stuffed mushrooms. All our goodies were crammed into Fridgey, awaiting a bit of rewarming on Christmas day. But on the morning of the 24th, we awoke to the *gunshot-loud* crackings of tree limbs breaking under the weight of a thick coating of ice. And because we live in the woods of New Kent, barely 30 feet from dense stands of trees in every direction, we weren't in the least surprised to learn the power was out—a frequent pitfall of having power lines near trees.

Turned out that the power outage affected thousands of homes spread across several states—and in more isolated areas (Hmm, let's see, *that* would be us.) the outage lasted weeks!! But we managed. We transferred our gourmet goodies to a big cooler, and on Christmas night, huddled about the fireplace, sitting in a room illuminated by hurricane lamps, we enjoyed a hot meal that included stuffed mushrooms!

How did we heat them? Well, Sparky is fueled by a huge propane tank behind our house. The local propane company keeps the tank topped off, so we've never run out of fuel. And the beauty of propane is that the pressure of the gas forces the fuel through the line and into our home, where it feeds our water-heater and Sparky.

All we had to do was turn on the gas knob, light the flame with a match, and Sparky came to life. We gently warmed the stuffed mushrooms and other foods in a covered skillet, and enjoyed a gourmet meal in the midst of a semi-disaster! So, in a pinch, our faithful Sparky came through, because he's powered by a dependable source of fuel—and the flow never stops!

In life, those who believe in and follow Christ are also powered by a dependable, never ending source of fuel. It's called God's Holy Spirit. When He walked the earth, Jesus said, "...I will ask the Father, and he will give you another Helper, to be with you forever...the Spirit of truth, whom the world cannot receive...." (John 14:16-17 ESV) The word helper comes from a Greek term that conveys the ideas of "advising, encouraging, comforting and strengthening": the basic survival gear needed to get through tough times.

With the power of the Holy Spirit we can make it through all of life's little disasters, whether they're ice storms or job layoffs or broken relationships. But we need to be careful to maintain the flow of the Holy Spirit's influence in our lives. There are certain things that can block the natural flow of this "fuel"; thoughts and actions that can crimp the gas-line, so to speak.

"For you have been called to live in freedom.... But don't use your freedom to satisfy your sinful nature. Instead, use your freedom to serve one another in love. ...But if you are always biting and devouring one another, watch out! Beware of destroying one another. ...Let the Holy Spirit guide your lives. Then you won't be doing what your sinful nature craves. The sinful nature wants to do evil, which is just the opposite of what the Spirit wants." (Galatians 5:13-17 NLT)

Keep the supply lines open: read and think on God's Word; talk to your Heavenly Father (praying about your fears, weaknesses and concerns, asking for His guidance, and always thanking Him for all He's done for you); and stay connected to other believers. When you do, you'll always have fresh supply of God's power and influence flowing into your life. You'll be able to weather any storm ... and even dine on gourmet stuffed mushrooms while you're waiting for it to pass!

Leeked Out:
The Truth about Onions!

Life, love, and leeks. What do they have in common? Glad you asked.

Leeks belong to the Allium genus of plants, which includes garlic, chives and onions. Since the onion is the most versatile and popular of these pseudo-veggies—sorry, dear friend Garlic!—and has an infamous reputation for being able to bring tears to the eyes of even the toughest of us, it's only fitting we now examine this important kitchen commodity.

Onions are chock full of Vitamins C, B1, B6, Potassium and fiber, which is why George Washington used to chow down on a raw onion whenever he felt a cold coming on. We're not sure if it warded off the cold, but it sure kept Martha away!

Trivia time: Way back in 1648, what was the first thing the Pilgrims planted in the New World? It certainly wasn't corn or pumpkins. And although Europeans brought their onions with them to North America, Native Americans already knew all about onions: they used them in cooking, medicinal poultices, and dyes!

Athletes in Ancient Greece ate lots of onions, believing they "balanced" the blood. Roman gladiators were rubbed down with onion juice to firm up their muscles, and in the Middle Ages, people could even pay their rent with onions. And doctors frequently prescribed onions to relieve headaches, coughs, snake bite and hair loss. And get this, the ancient Egyptians actually worshipped the onion! They believed its spherical shape and concentric rings symbolized eternal life.

Which reminds us, we promised to compare onions to life and love, didn't we? Let's list some similarities. First, like life and relationships (the "love" part of our post), the onion takes many differing forms. There are common onions, available in three colors (yellow onions, red onions, white onions). There are wild onions, spring onions, scallions, and pearl onions. Onions come fresh, frozen, dehydrated, and canned. They can be chopped, pickled, caramelized, minced, and even granulated. All this variety, all this utility, reminds us of the diverseness of relationships, and the many turns life can take.

And like an onion, life and people have multiple layers. Our experiences in this world are like periodically peeling back another layer of the "onion" to reveal new mysteries, new opportunities, new lessons. And the same can be said of relationships: in order to truly get to know someone—and to fully understand why we do the strange, idiosyncratic things that we all do—we again need to peel back the layers that insulate people from people.

Onions and Life are fascinating and many splendored things! So are onions and people!

How numerous are your works, LORD! You have made them all wisely; the earth is filled with your creations.
—Psalm 104:124 ISV

Who's Bugging You?

Each spring brings dozens of Ruby-throated Hummingbirds to our humble abode in the woods. They arrive by the dozens, and they consume nectar by the gallons! No exaggeration here, we go through at least a quart of sugar water each day.

(Hummers need their calories!)

We brew our own nectar to keep up with the demand: 1 part sugar, 4 parts water, brought to a boil for two minutes to kill all the bacteria these little fellas. We to room temperature another tasty recipe Woodhaven.) that's harmful to then cool the nectar before serving. (Just for hungry guests at

Trouble is, it's not just the hummingbirds that crave sweet stuff. There are thousands of greedy ants—actually, *hundreds* of thousands—in the surrounding woods, and they apparently have radar tuned to the aroma of nectar bubbling on the range. These industrious pests will climb a two-story brick wall and work their way through the tiniest crack in a window to get their share, too. And although we scrupulously clean our kitchen counters of every single drop of hummingbird syrup, somehow the ants know that we're constantly preparing the stuff inside. And they never stop trying to get in.

Imagine the trouble that ants could make, the hassle of getting rid of them, the loss of our peace of mind ... only they AIN'T getting in. They make it up the brick, to the windowsill, but aren't able to trespass any further, because we periodically spray along the base of the kitchen window with ant poison. (Hey, we all have to go sometime.)

The ant spray lays down a line of chemicals these pesky intruders can't cross. We essentially put up an invisible boundary that tells the ants "This far, and no further!" It's like a News Flash for insects: *Attention all ants! No, you can't come into our kitchen and take over!*

And yet, we mustn't lose sight of the bigger picture. Ants are vital to the balance of God's ecology. They control other pests, carry seed, and create healthy soil. Still, they have no business invading your home. And know what? Sometimes people behave just like ants! They have immense value, but they often try and work their way into areas of our lives where they have no business being!

Do you have any "ants" in your life? People who want to intrude and take over? If you do, have you considered establishing some boundaries? We're not saying people are pests. But they can be pesky at times. And greedy and intrusive and troublesome and hard to get rid of. And they can steal your peace if you allow it. *Just saying.*

We love people, and we hope you do, too. We also enjoy encouraging and helping them when they need it; but people (until they allow God to *fully* work in their lives and transform them) tend to be selfish and self-centered. If allowed to, some will try to hog your time, abuse your willingness to help and serve, invade your privacy, manipulate your emotions, exploit your gifts—basically control your life!

But people, like ants, are a fact of life. Ya just gotta learn how to deal with them. That means setting boundaries. In other words, drawing invisible lines in our lives that say "this far and no further"!

Yes, we are commanded to "Share each other's burdens, and in this way obey the law of Christ." (Galatians 6:2 NLT) However, God NEVER intended us to allow others to control us! Just as the problem of beneficial ants is answered with BALANCE, so too is the issue of dealing with people. Balance is key: "Let each of you look not only to his own interests, but also to the interests of others." (Philippians 2:4 ESV)

Christian authors Dr. Henry Cloud and Dr. John Townsend explain in their book, *Boundaries: When to Say Yes, How to Say No*, "Just as homeowners set physical property lines around their land, we need to set mental, physical, emotional and spiritual boundaries for our lives to help us distinguish what is our responsibility and what is not." (Page 13)

We always want to be loving, accepting and helpful, but there are some problems we can't fix, some needs we cannot or *should* not meet. And even when we can help solve things, we need to remember that we're only human and that our time and resources, as well as our physical and emotional energies, are limited.

So every time we say *YES* to something, we're automatically saying *NO* to something else. We also need to learn how to distinguish between people's "needs" and "desires"! And we need to develop the confidence to *just say NO!*

If we fail to set boundaries, someone will always have us jumping at their every whim and cry, and we'll end up constantly stressed out and frustrated with life. Eventually, we burn out! People, whether unintentionally or not, can keep us from achieving our own everyday goals and, ultimately, fulfilling our dreams.

If we fail to set some boundaries, people can even keep us from doing the work God wants us to do! So, drawing the line is not being selfish. To the contrary, the "...Goal of learning boundaries is to free us up to protect, nurture and develop the lives God has given us stewardship over." (*Boundaries*, p. 285)

Stop letting people constantly bug you! Stop allowing them to invade places in your lives where they have no business. Stop letting them eat up all your time and energy. Jesus said, "...You will know the truth, and the truth will set you free." (John 8:32 ESV) Let us "spray"!

Delectable Duos!

Ever notice how certain foods work really well together? Like bread and butter. Rice and beans. Cream and sugar. Biscuits and gravy. Peaches and cream. Salt and pepper. Lettuce and tomatoes. Peanut butter and jelly. We call these pairings of food *delectable duos!* We've only listed a few, but our list could go on and on. And we've probably started you thinking about a few of your own favorite *culinary couplings.*

Although any of the items listed above can stand alone,  and although each one has individual value and can fill a need all by itself, bringing two of them together greatly increases the appeal and value. Peanut butter is a good source of protein, but it can be a little dry and a little blah. Jelly is fruity and sweet, but it's not very filling. Either one works well as a sandwich spread, but just ask any kid: mix the two and you have a nutritious sandwich that tastes like a snack! Because these two foodstuffs are BETTER TOGETHER!

Bet you already guessed *this* kitchen wisdom: there are tons of great examples of things in life that work well together. Spices, such as brown sugar and cinnamon. Foods, such as apple pie and vanilla ice cream.

And how about comedy teams, such as Abbot and Costello, or Laurel and Hardy. Musical duos, such as Donny and Marie (okay, forget that one), or Simon and Garfunkel. (And by the way, did Art Garfunkel ever do anything noteworthy while he was on his own? Just curious.)

People can *always* work together to do amazing things. You, us, and them, too.

No one is an island. God created people to be relational beings: to have interaction with Him, obviously, but also to interact with those around us. "...The Lord God said, 'It is not good for the man to be alone.'" (Genesis 2:18 HCSB) Although this verse relates to marriage, the first institution God created, its wisdom applies to ALL relationships.

The Bible is full of relationships. Actually, it's *all* about relationships. And it's *the* Book of God's relationship to us! God knows us better than anyone, and what He knows is that *we need relationships*. Every human being has a basic need and desire to love and be loved, to share, to communicate, to socialize. Even the grumpiest, seemingly most unapproachable person needs to talk to someone! Perhaps that's why social media is so popular today.

Two people working together are better able to achieve their goals and realize their dreams, because there is power in two people who are mutually supportive and accountable; two people who can encourage and assist each other. That's what the "buddy system" is all about. That's why there are support groups such as AA, and mentoring groups such as Big Brothers and Big Sisters. That's why a prayer partner can help keep us tuned in to God; and why corporations hope you have a "best friend" at work. Such connections make work more bearable, and life more enjoyable.

Please don't face life alone. "Two people are better off than one, for they can help each other succeed." (Ecclesiastes 4:9 NLT) "...One person (can) chase a thousand... (but) two people put ten thousand to flight...." (Deuteronomy 32:30 NLT)

So find a friend, whether online, on the job, at your local congregation, or right next door. And don't forget that the Lord also wants to partner with you in every endeavor.

Palatable Pairings!

We've just discussed things in the kitchen that work great together, by listing such "palatable pairings" as peaches and cream, or peanut butter and jelly—and how the Power of Two can carry over into life. When two people work together to achieve a goal or realize a dream, they can accomplish far more than they might individually. The *sum* really *is* greater than the parts. That's why the buddy system works so well— on the job, when dieting, cleaning the house, etc. And it usually makes things a lot more fun, too!

Here's a few more examples of kitchen companions: fork and knife (only together can they conquer that juicy steak); cup and saucer (both serve a need, but only together are they an elegant couple); table and chair (Who wants to eat standing up? And once you're seated, you'll realize a table can hold far more dishes than your lap!); pot and lid. (Hey, do we really need to explain this dynamic duo?)

There's a Biblical basis for the Power of Two, one that goes well beyond all those cute animal couples that boarded Noah's Ark "two by two"! (Genesis 6:9) Yes, the Power of Two has a spiritual application: the GOD Factor! What's the GOD Factor? *Well*, we just now made that part up. But essentially, it describes higher mathematics. (*Higher* as in Heavenly). It's when $1 + 1 = 3$. Here's how it works: "...Where two or three gather together as My followers, I am there among them." (Matthew 18:20 NLT) In other words, when believers meet to fellowship or pray together, God joins the gathering!

$$1 + 1 = 3$$

Prior to the coming of Jesus Christ (Yeshua), it took 12 men to form a "proper" spiritual gathering or assembly. Thanks to the presence of the Lord, it takes only two now! (Actually, only ONE, but we'll get to that.) It takes only two, because God shows up—*and He carries more weight!!* He's the "CEO" in any meeting and He has the authority to get things done—even when there's not a quorum.

But to ensure our team leader is present, we need to be sure we're allowing Him to be in charge. We have to invite Him to be the captain of our souls, to take the helm of our lives, and chart the right course for each of us. After all, He should be in charge, because He's infinitely wiser and more powerful than we are. He's our safe port in a storm: "What shall we say about such wonderful things as these? If God is for us, who can ever be against us?" (Romans 8:31 NLT)

"Wait a minute!" you may be thinking. "What if I'm all by my lonesome? What then? Does God abandon me so He can go hang out in a 'crowd' of two or more?" *No way!* When it comes to a relationship with God, *One* is NOT the loneliest number! God is always in the midst of "two or more," but He's also *constantly* at the side of every SINGLE person! In fact, He's "...a friend who sticks closer than a brother." (Proverbs 18:24 NIV)

You may be single and feeling like you don't have any real friends; you may be divorced or widowed, and struggling with isolation and despair; you may be an orphan, or at times you feel like one; someone may have abandoned you or left you in the lurch; you may feel all alone in this big world, but God "Himself has said, 'I will never desert you, nor will I forsake you.'" (Hebrews 13:8 NASB)

With Christ, you are never alone! "...Remember I am with you always until the end of time." (Matthew 28:20 GWT) So whether you're "alone" or in a group, tap into the Power of Two!

...Do not fear, for I am with you; do not be dismayed,
for I am your God. I will strengthen you and help you;
I will uphold you with my righteous right hand.
—Isaiah 41:10 NIV

Culinary Oddballs!

No, "Culinary Oddballs" is not the title of a new sitcom about a couple of kooky cooks; instead, we're discussing those freaky food misfits frequently found in the kitchen: fruits and veggies that have the chutzpah to be *different!* These curious culinary nonconformists keep us on our toes; just when we think we know them, we often learn something new and surprising.

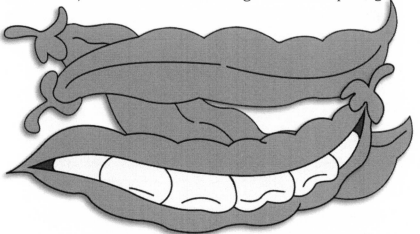

Veggies are many and varied. Although most people agree that veggies are the edible parts of plants, the actual classification of vegetable varies slightly from culture to culture. Carrots and turnips are roots, celery and asparagus are stalks and stems, and spinach and lettuce are leaves. What's a tomato?

Tomatoes go great in salads, hanging out with all the other veggies; but this red rascal isn't actually a veggie, at all. The misunderstood tomato belongs to the fruit category. So, one might wonder why grocers don't display the tomatoes side by side with the apples and strawberries. Perhaps it's because—unlike his fellow fruit—the nonconformist tomato doesn't make great jam or taste very good in a pie.

When pondering veggies, the avocado is another of the usual suspects. But again, it belongs to the fruit category. Peas? When we used to leave these little green guys on our plates, our mommies would say, "Eat your veggies!" Alas, peas belong to the category of seeds and nuts. Weird? Well, we are talking about something that lies dormant in a pod until some unsuspecting person comes along and.... No, wait! We've got peas confused with those green pod-things from *Invasion of the Body Snatchers*!

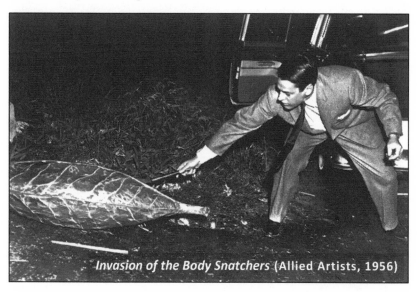

Invasion of the Body Snatchers (Allied Artists, 1956)

Coconuts? They're also seeds. Really, *really*, big seeds. Who knew? But all this just goes to demonstrate, in the kitchen there are certain culinary oddballs that don't conform, don't necessarily fit in with the rest of their group, and are generally misunderstood. Do we neglect them? No, because they're tasty, and we find ways to help them fit in.

In life, just as in the kitchen, we continually encounter social misfits. People who for various reasons don't quite fit in with the rest of the crowd. Maybe these people think or dress differently, maybe they're just shy, maybe they simply have different beliefs, interests, goals and dreams.

Have you ever felt like an oddball? Maybe at school, or at work, or even in your own family? Cheer up, and welcome to the human race. We've all been there. In fact, some of us never left! But being an oddball isn't necessarily a bad thing.

Most intelligent, creative and fun people often come across as a little different. And even the most popular and well-adjusted individuals eventually find themselves sticking out like sore thumbs in certain situations, or when among certain groups of people. None of this means we can't toss ourselves together to make a social salad.

Face facts: sooner or later someone's going to misunderstand you, and miscategorize you. It's okay. You're not alone. So relax and learn to be comfortable in your own skin. Repeat after us, "Thank you [God] for making me so wonderfully complex! Your workmanship is marvelous—how well I know it." (Psalm 139:14 NLT)

Remember that you have GREAT value. After all, God sacrificed His only Son, Jesus Christ, in order to redeem you! And once you're a believer, you will always be an important part of God's family: "...He hath made us accepted in the beloved." (Ephesians 1:6 KJB)

What shall we say about such wonderful things as these?
If God is for us, who can ever be against us?
—Romans 8:31 NLT

A Strategy for Salads

In "Culinary Oddballs!" we discussed those misfit foods that defy categorization. For instance, most vegetables are either roots, stems, seeds or leaves, but the tomato...well, it's not even classed as a veggie. It belongs to the fruit family. So does the avocado. Yes, you've been scooping up *fruit* dip with those tortilla chips. And the coconut? Another fruit, right? *Nah*, coconuts are actually really big seeds, and therefore fit better in the seed and nut category.

How about peas? They're just plain *weird*—hiding in their green pods all quiet and unassuming, all the while plotting to take over the earth. (Like in the movie *Invasion of the Body Snatchers*.)

On the other hand, no one is fooled by the banana, right? Bananas are fruit, period! Banana cream pie, banana ice cream, bananas dipped in chocolate, Bananas Foster, banana pudding! And yet ... the plantain belongs to the same family as the banana, but in many cultures the plantain is prepared and served as a veggie. In fact, it's often considered the "Hispanic potato." In several Latin American cuisines, plantains are baked, boiled, mashed, and fried—just like spuds. And by the way, we prefer *tostones* (crispy fried and salted sliced plantains) over French fries! So, is the plantain a fruit or a veggie? *Uh*, yeah.

What do we do with these culinary oddballs? We enjoy them. We find ways to use them and help them fit in to our meals. We give the tomato a big group hug between two slices of rye with some baked ham; we blend the avocado with seasonings and make a killer dip that tortilla chips can't resist; we sprinkle coconut on everything from shrimp to ice cream, and sometimes we lovingly smother it in dark chocolate; and peas... well, now that we're adults we love them, too! And all these items can be tossed together in a salad or stew!

We also encounter "oddballs" in life. Good people that don't seem to fit the standard profile. People with their own unique personalities, gifts and talents. People who have much to offer and contribute—if we let them. Maybe they have different beliefs, interests, or backgrounds. Maybe they're just shy. But for one reason or another, they don't fit in with the crowd. And know what? At one time or another, in some situation or group, we've all been there!

What should we do with these social misfits? Toss 'em out? Nope. Toss 'em *in!* Make a social salad! How do we do that? By being welcoming and accepting and inclusive. Here's God's simple recipe for making a Social Salad. It's really quite simple:

SYMPATHIZE!
Remember what it was like when *you* felt alone and strange —like you didn't fit in; like you were an oddball! Then treat others the same way you wish you'd been treated. Welcome them. Make them feel accepted and a part of your group, circle, etc. "You are not to wrong or oppress an alien [newcomer/ misfit/ 'oddball'], because you were aliens ['oddballs'] in the land of Egypt." (Exodus 22:21 ISV)

STRATEGIZE!
Think of ways to use their gifts and talents, ways to help them feel comfortable with the rest of the crowd. Help them find a place to fit in. "The stranger [newcomer/misfit/'oddball'] who resides with you shall be to you as the native among you, and you shall love him as yourself, for you were aliens ['oddballs'] in the land of Egypt." (Leviticus 19:34 NASB)

SOCIALIZE!
Do we need to explain this one? Just talk. Communicate. Be friendly. Share food, fun, and fellowship. Play nice together! "...Show your love for the alien [newcomer/misfit/'oddball'],

for you were aliens ['oddballs'] in the land of Egypt." (Deuteronomy 10:19 NASB)

If you feel awkward or uncomfortable (or odd!) doing any of this, it's probably because you're fearful of coming across as an oddball yourself—which is a sure sign that you really *do* understand what it's like. And if you understand ... *well* ... then you're the best person to make a social salad using the "3-S" recipe!

No Bundt!

Let's discuss molds. No, not the fuzzy green ones that grow on very old bread—the kind used to shape stuff, such as jello.

We have several molds designed to shape different foods, and we have a lot of fun using them. We have a heart-shaped baking pan, and we've used it to bake a meatloaf that screams "Love"! We have molds for shaping mounds of rice and chicken salad, making a beautiful presentation when serving these dishes. We have ice cube trays that enable us to freeze punch in a variety of cute shapes. And we have a fish mold, too! So if our doctor ever tells us to cut out red meat and go on a seafood diet, we'll just bake a meatloaf shaped like a fish.

In addition to all these cool molds, there's also the universally familiar ring-shaped Bundt baking pan. The Bundt design mimics the form of a traditional European cake called *Gugelhupf*, which was popular with Jewish communities in Germany, Austria and Poland. The first Bundt pans were marketed in the U.S. in the late 1950s. The pans quickly caught on, and today you can buy Bundt pans in a variety of designs, including cathedrals and city skylines—because who doesn't want to play Godzilla and devour a whole city made of cake?

Even Godzilla knows ya gotta floss. (Toho Studios, 1954)

Interestingly, a Gugelhupf is baked from a specific, yeast-based recipe with fruit and nuts. You can't say the same thing about a Bundt cake. In fact, there are no recipes for Bundt cake. So what exactly *is* a Bundt cake? Simple: anything you bake in a Bundt pan. It doesn't matter if it's lemon cake or angel food; if it contains fruit, nuts, or a tunnel of fudge filling; whatever goes into a Bundt pan is called a Bundt cake. Which provides a perfect analogy for what we want to share.

Although Bundt cakes retain the flavors baked into them, they nevertheless lose part of their identity. Being molded by a Bundt pan makes them Bundt cakes. A chocolate cake becomes a Bundt cake. Same for yellow cake, banana cake, or what have you. If cakes could talk, they'd probably argue with the cook about being baked in a mold that leads to the loss of their individuality! (Can you guess where we're going with this?)

People often end up like Bundt cakes. They may start out as chocolate, vanilla, yellow, or red velvet, but somewhere in life they allow the world to mold them into something generic.

This world is continually pressuring people to conform to a certain image and mindset. Peer pressure is constantly working to mold us; the need to fit in or the desire to "keep up with the Joneses" are just two examples of "social Bundt pans." And if you're a follower of Christ, you face even more pressure to conform to secular society. Face it, "Bundt people" want you to join their ranks.

The Apostle Paul admonishes us, "Do not conform to the pattern of this world, but be transformed by the renewing of your mind." (Romans 12:2 NIV) In other words, don't allow this fallen, negative, lost and hopeless world to squeeze you

into its mold. Instead, be different. Hold to a higher standard. Avoid the dog-eat-dog mentality of the rest of society. Be like Christ: never stoop to the low standards of people who are unforgiving and vindictive, unloving and often vicious; take the high road; rise above your circumstances and whatever else the world throws at you; and live by faith!

Get God's perspective on life by reading His Word. Trade in any hopeless, faithless feelings you may have, for God's faithful promises. Replace any negative, hateful, selfish, stinking thinking with the "mind of Christ" and "love, joy, peace, patience, kindness, goodness, faithfulness, gentleness, and self-control." (Galatians 5:22-23 NLT)

Don't be a Bundt! Be *better!* Think *different* and live victoriously! "With perfect peace You will protect those whose minds cannot be changed, because they trust You." (Isaiah 26:3 GWT)

Spic and Span!

Roman author, naturalist, and philosopher "Pliny the Elder" (AD 23–August 25, AD 79) once stated, "Home is where the heart is." How true! And all the modern-day gurus of interior design frequently add that "the kitchen is the heart of the home"! Fair enough.

In the same way that blood flows from the human heart, nourishing the body, frequent meals come from the kitchen, sustaining the household. And when you invite people over, if allowed to roam freely, that's where your guests tend to gather. People want to hang out with you in the kitchen. Everyone knows, whether your kitchen is big or small, *that's where the action is!*

Before we go any further, let us reassure you: it's not what's in your kitchen that's important, it's what comes out of your kitchen. A humble heart can supply a whole lot of love! Also, your kitchen doesn't need to be stocked with all the latest gadgets or high-tech appliances to be functional; nor do you need hand-rubbed custom cabinets or those highly coveted countertops of polished granite. You absolutely DO need to keep your kitchen clean!!!

Besides the health hazards of a dirty kitchen, face it, nobody wants to wake up to an ugly mess. It's not at all appetizing to have a cup of coffee and a Danish in a nasty kitchen. And after all, that's where you prepare the food that you and the people you care about will be eating! Would you want to eat in a restaurant famous for keeping a dirty kitchen? *Yuck!* In fact, restaurant kitchens are periodically inspected by the health department for cleanliness, and if one repeatedly doesn't pass muster, the owner is forced to close until he or she cleans up their act. (Literally!)

Back to the home: On a recent *Dr. Oz* program, experts acknowledged that the kitchen was often the dirtiest room in the house! (Yes, even dirtier than the bathroom!) Even in the "cleanest" kitchens, the ones where the cooks always wash their hands and carefully preserve and prepare their foods, there was... (cue the creepy music) ...*nastiness* unseen by the human eye! (Oh, the horror!) When kitchen surfaces were viewed under a microscope, experts discovered germs and bacteria lurking in corners and crevices. And one huge source of bacteria? The always damp sponge used to wash the dishes was a breeding ground for the little buggers!

Now mind you, these kitchens looked and smelled clean; the people maintaining them were careful and conscientious and thought they were doing a good job. But under closer scrutiny their kitchens—the hearts of their homes—had all their dirty little secrets brought to light! (Now, if you haven't guessed already, we're about to compare the kitchen, with all its invisible bacteria and germs lurking about, to the human heart. *Cough!*)

There are a lot of nasty little critters breeding in our hearts. Every one of us needs to take steps daily to keep our hearts sanitized, and hence, healthy. Like our kitchens, we all harbor dirty little secrets, often undetected because we simply don't take time to thoroughly examine our hearts. Harmful parasites such as wrongful attitudes (prejudice, bigotry, jealousy, envy, strife, selfishness, self-centeredness, pride—*hello!*—and numerous other mindsets, so please feel free to fill in the blank) as well as unbelief. Sometimes a slight, whether intentional or not, can lead to a person holding a grudge. If not dealt with, a grudge leads to bitterness, and bitterness is a silent killer of the heart!

Sanitizing a kitchen calls for strong measures such as ammonia and bleach (*Um*, but not at the same time!); getting your heart spic and span calls for similar measures. The idiom "spic and span" comes from root words and imagery suggesting fresh, clean wood and the new beams of a sound sailing vessel. King David understood the need to keep his heart spic and span. He must have done a pretty good job at it, too, because God describes the poet and soldier by saying, "I have found that David ... is a man after my own heart, who will carry out all my wishes." (Acts 13:22 ISV)

So King David must have been perfect, right? If you believe that, we have some swampland in Florida we'd like to sell you. Check out 1st and 2nd Samuel and try to remember you're not reading *Peyton Place*! But David *was* loyal and devoted to God. He knew he made mistakes, but he was totally honest with himself and with God. He wasn't malicious and he always tried to do his best. In other words, his heart was in the right place.

David examined his life daily and asked God to help him in all things. We need to do the same. Read what David wrote in Psalm 51. Spend quality time with the Lord every day and make it your prayer. Here's just one precious verse from the chapter: "Create in me a clean heart, O God (and) renew a loyal spirit within me." (Psalm 51:10 NLT)

David is essentially asking God to help him keep his heart spic and span! Let's each ask God to do the same for our own hearts.

What's Cookin'?

Pillsbury once had an ad slogan declaring, "Nothing says lovin' like something from the oven!" And we all know that "the way to a man's heart is through his stomach." Expressing love through food is an American tradition.

We've acknowledged that the kitchen is the heart of the home. Just as our physical hearts pump the blood that sustains our bodies, our kitchens sustain our families, both nutritionally and emotionally, with a steady flow of home-cooked meals. Even if you take your meals away from home, somebody's kitchen is keeping you alive, whether it's at a restaurant, college cafeteria, or the factory kitchen that prepares those frozen dinners we all eat in a pinch. So, if you love food, ya gotta love the kitchen, too. It's where our meals are cooked, and the place where we most often enjoy them. It's also a great starting point for expressing love.

While she was still with us, we'd often visit Tom's *Grandma*. How does that old song go? "Over the river and through the woods to grandmother's house we go...." You know the rest. Except for the part about the horse and sleigh, the song pretty much described the long trip to her house: three hours of tree-lined highway and the occasional billboard hawking fireworks or little pecan pies.

Grandma's home was small. The rooms were distinguished by old furnishings and outdated decor. Whenever we visited, we always ended up in her kitchen; it's where she overfed us, and where we sat for hours, stuffed, happy, and chatting across the table. Grandma's table was set with mix-matched dishes, paper napkins, and oddly-placed silverware, all atop a tablecloth that really didn't go with anything. Her meals were simple fare, the Southern food Tom had grown up with, but... *Ooh! How delicious!*

Being a Northerner, Wilma was thrilled by the awesome taste and crispiness of her fried pork chops. "It's just her usual hearty fare," Tom would say nonchalantly. "She breads the chops with crushed, seasoned, cornflakes." Her "usual fare," the meal she had prepared with no fuss and no pretension, tasted absolutely gourmet. It was simply divine! When Wilma asked her where she got the recipe, Grandma simply shrugged and said she couldn't rightly remember: "I was just using what I had in the cupboard." Now, obviously there was a little something extra in that cupboard. Can you guess what it was?

What Grandma lacked in decor—what she never even knew about "style"—she made up for, with something far more precious: *her love.*

There's a simple truth here. Please don't miss it. "Better is a dinner of herbs where love is, than a fatted calf and hatred." (Proverbs 15:17 NKJV)

Sounds cryptic? Here's another translation: "A vegetarian meal served with love is better than a big, thick steak with a plateful of animosity." (ISV)

The secret ingredient in any good recipe is LOVE. When served with love, even the simplest, humblest meal turns into a banquet. What's for dinner? Same thing we served last night and every day before: Love. Whatever you're cooking up today, prepare it lovingly and it will be a culinary masterpiece!

Remember those twin pops you ate when you were a kid? You'd break one down the middle to get two single pops, one for you and one for a friend. Didn't they taste so much better when shared? Food and love go together like biscuits 'n' gravy! (Okay, we need to stop making everybody hungry!)

If you really want to make a friend, go to someone's house and eat with him ... the people who give you their food give you their heart.

—Cesar Chavez

Looking for the Label?

One of the first things you want to do in the kitchen is label stuff. When you don't, you're in for trouble. Some things look almost the same but are actually very different.

White vinegar, bleach and ammonia are all thin, clear liquids commonly found in the kitchen. So, if you have an unlabeled bottle filled with clear liquid, it's hard to know exactly what it is. If you mix it with a little olive oil, you have a 33% chance of coming up with salad dressing. You also have about a 67% chance of needing to have your stomach pumped.

Things actually wouldn't go that far. Minus the label, you'd probably be smart enough to test the stuff to determine exactly what it is. This takes some thinking, though. Let's see, you could dab a bit in your hair: if it doesn't go white, then it's probably not bleach. You could give the stuff a good sniff: if it makes your head feel like it's about to explode, and brings torrents of tears to your eyes, then it's probably ammonia. Other lookalikes that aren't *taste*-alikes: sugar and salt; flour, cornstarch and baking soda. If they weren't labeled, we'd have to figure out what's what.

Some things look different but are quite similar. White pepper is just as peppery as regular black pepper; and a brown egg tastes the same as its paler counterpart—both make a nice omelet. But brown eggs are brown, and white pepper is usually labeled as such. Face it, in the kitchen, we NEED our labels. When things are labeled we don't have to think; we don't need to test or figure stuff out. We can relax and turn our brains off.

One of the last things you want to do in the world is label people. *When you do, you're in for trouble. Some people look almost the same but are actually very different. Some people look different but are quite similar.*

So we need to figure out what's what—or rather, who's who. Face it, in the kitchen, we need our labels. When it comes to people, we WANT our labels. When people are labeled, we don't have to think; we don't need to try and figure them out. <u>We can relax and turn our brains off</u>.

Avoid the temptation: don't label people! We need to approach every person as a unique individual—not as someone we've prejudged, categorized and labeled. Some of the labels we resort to out of laziness include black, white, Asian, male, female, Republican, Democrat, good, bad, thin, fat, smart, and blonde. (*Aha*, see how stupid labels sound?)

Labeling people is easier than getting to know them. Labeling people gives us an excuse to either interact with them or simply dismiss them. Labeling people limits our own options and demeans the person being labeled. It's counterproductive—and it's destructive.

Since labels help us keep "stuff" in its proper place, we assume that labeling people will help us do the same. We mark people as stupid or wise, helpful or worthless, givers or takers, etc., etc.! More times than not, our labels are incorrect. That blonde is a brain surgeon, the guy in the raggedy jeans is a business tycoon, the little old lady in the drugstore is a champion mud wrestler, those two suspicious-looking dudes staking out your neighborhood are Mormons, and that geeky kid with the thick glasses—the one who looks like the next Apple CEO—well, he's just extremely nearsighted.

Gender, ethnicity (we never use the term race as a distinguishing characteristic, because we all belong to the same race: the human race), political affiliations, economic status, geographic origin, educational background and religious belief should never be used to label and limit people.

Do you like being labeled and categorized? Nobody does. We sure don't. We never like it when someone feels they have us pegged, that they know what makes us tick and what we can and cannot accomplish. But we make allowances for these label-makers, "for they know not what they do!" We also try our best not to follow their example. Labels are for peas and pepper—not people.

"There is neither Jew nor Greek, there is neither bond nor free, there is neither male nor female: for you are all one in Christ Jesus." (Galatians 3:28 KJ 2000)

> *Don't just pretend to love others. Really love them.*
> *Hate what is wrong. Hold tightly to what is good.*
> —Romans 12:9 NLT

Are You Putting Me On?

When working in the kitchen, we usually put on an apron to protect our clothing. The last thing we want is to get a big grease spot on a nice shirt or blouse. It wouldn't exactly help our fashion image to wear stained duds to church or a dinner engagement. Sometimes we get in a hurry and forgo this simple piece of protective wear, and those tend to be the very occasions when something spatters on us. So we've learned from past mishaps that putting on an apron is a lot easier than removing a stain—and takes less time, too!

There are other things we frequently wear in the kitchen, such as oven mitts. We wouldn't dare reach into a 450-degree oven without this thermal protection on our hands. Well, at some point, we probably *did* reach in with our sensitive bare pinkies—but only once! As in life, some things are too hot to handle on your own. So we use potholders to remove lids, because when a pot gets hot and pressure builds inside, it tends to let off steam—like a few of our friends. No, we don't want any steam burns. And when washing dishes, we put on Playtex gloves. Being exposed to abrasive soap pads during extended sessions of scrubbing, can be rough on the hands. And we don't want to become calloused.

We're making an analogy again. Of course we are! That's what we do best in Angel in the Kitchen. So, are there things we can put on in life, when dealing with people, when handling sensitive situations, which can similarly protect us? You bet! Romans 13:14 admonishes us to "...Put on the Lord Jesus Christ, and make no provision for the flesh." (ESV)

What does it mean to "put on Christ"? It means adopting His attitudes about life and people. Jesus is loving and patient with us, and He wants us to act the same way toward others. Putting on Christ is the opposite of having a negative, resentful, grumpy, downright nasty attitude. Wear the latter out in public, and waitresses and dogs will avoid you like the plague. Putting on Christ—putting on an attitude of love—will protect your disposition, which in turn will protect your relationships, your job, your interactions at the market, as well as your reputation and your witness for Christ. Hence, your good character won't be stained.

Instead of being defensive and ready to bite the heads off defenseless chickens and babies, putting on a meek and humble attitude can prevent singed feelings when handling friends, family and coworkers. When constantly dealing with abrasive people, putting on an attitude of compassion and understanding can protect you becoming calloused. "...Love covers a multitude of sins." (1 Peter 4:8 NASB)

We particularly like Romans 13:14 in the New Living Translation: "Instead, clothe yourself in the presence of the Lord Jesus Christ." Being in the "presence" of Christ means you'll also be adorned with His strength and clothed in His grace—so you'll be dressed to handle hot situations and deal with coarse people. Oh, and you'll be stain-resistant, as well.

So when in the kitchen, put on your apron and oven mitts; and in life, put on Christ. Wear a smile and adopt His attitude of Godly Love toward people. What does Godly Love look like? Read 1 Corinthians 13 to find out.

Got a Light?

Have you ever had trouble finding something in a kitchen cabinet because all the labels were shrouded in shadows? Have you ever scrubbed furiously to remove a stain from a dinner plate, only to realize later that it's a blemish in the plate itself? Have you ever had difficultly reading a cookbook laid open on the kitchen countertop? Responding yes to any of these, could be an indication that your kitchen has insufficient lighting.

Assuming there's nothing wrong with your eyesight, the lights in your kitchen may be too few, or improperly placed, or simply not emitting enough bright light. And most cooks agree, there's nothing more frustrating than working in a dimly lit kitchen where you can't see what you're doing.

You can have the latest, most expensive "designer kitchen," but if it's poorly lit, you've just wasted your money. You won't be able to see which spices you're sprinkling into the soup, or how badly you're bleeding after accidentally slicing open your finger while dicing onions because you couldn't see!

A great kitchen has lights everywhere: over the stove, over the sink, above every foot of counter space. And if you have an island, over that too. There are even lights for *under* the counters and *inside* the cabinets! You need to be able to see what's lurking under the sink! But lights aren't just for function. Good lighting adds to the esthetics of both the kitchen and dining area. In fact, a handsome light fixture properly positioned above the table, such as a chandelier, is just as important as your place-settings and centerpiece.

Form and function. Lights are useful tools that add beauty to life. It's close to impossible to get along without light, but light is something you rarely think about until you have to do without it. Living in the woods of New Kent, we've had many occasions when we lost power. And when it gets dark in the woods ... it *really* gets dark! So we've stocked up on candles, flashlights, and hurricane lamps. Sitting in the dark is no fun, and a world without light would be a dark and gloomy place.

In society, light promotes safety and order. (If you don't believe this, read your history: people seem to go crazy during blackouts in major metropolitan areas. When the light goes out, the looting and vandalism starts.) Lights illuminate and guide our way. (Streetlamps and fluorescent signs.) They control and direct traffic, further ensuring order. (Traffic and crossing lights.) We could go on, but we think you get the point.

The Bible explains that God and His holy Word are the ultimate source of Spiritual Light. Jesus said, "I am the light of the world. If you follow me, you won't have to walk in darkness, because you will have the light that leads to life." (John 8:12 NLT) "Your Word is a lamp to guide my feet and a light for my path." (Psalm 119:105 NLT)

This Divine Spiritual Light serves the same purpose as natural and man-made lights: it illuminates the truth and guides our ways; it brings beauty to life; it promotes order and safety; it directs all human activity. And without God's Word, this world would be a dark and gloomy place. Funny thing is, just like natural and man-made lights, we often don't miss the illuminating, organizing, cheering, reassuring, and safety-promoting effects of God's Word until it's taken away from society. People living in countries where Judeo-Christian beliefs have been banned, know this truth well.

One last thought: When the sun goes down and the house grows dark, we switch on a light. Flashlights and candles bring light into the darkest corners of a room. In life, we're to be God's spiritual flashlights and candles, helping to dispel darkness wherever we go. In His famous Sermon on the Mount, Jesus told His followers, "You are the light of the world—like a city on a hilltop that cannot be hidden. No one lights a lamp and then puts it under a basket. Instead, a lamp is placed on a stand, where it gives light to everyone in the house. In the same way, let your good deeds shine out for all to see...." (Matthew 5:14-16 NLT)

The All-Purpose Cleaner

Bleach is our best friend in the kitchen. Yes, it's great for brightening whites in the laundry, but it's also a versatile all-purpose cleaner. Bleach seems to remove any stain, no matter how stubborn. It cuts through grease. And it disinfects, too!

Pretend for a moment that you're in one of those cheap 1950s sci-fi movies and civilization as we know it suddenly grinds to a halt. You'll want your bottle of bleach handy: just a drop in a tankful of stagnant water will chlorinate it and kill all the harmful bugs. So even if the TV is useless, and there's no cell phone service, you'll still have plenty of clean water to drink as you contemplate rebuilding civilization—or simply returning to nature to run free with the wildlife.

In the meantime, we use our bleach to kill and remove mildew under the sink. It also removes grime from our kitchen cabinets. And it cuts through grease and cleans Tupperware better than anything else we've used. In fact, bleach removes those creepy red stains that are always left after microwaving a plastic container of chili or spaghetti sauce.

And if you're like us and have a white refrigerator,

bleach is great for removing those incriminating little finger smudges left by kids sneaking an ice cream bar or the last piece of lemon meringue pie.

We also use bleach to disinfect the cutting board and the kitchen sponge we use to wash the dishes. The beauty of bleach is that it deep cleans, removes stubborn stains, purifies and sanitizes! And if a lock of hair should fall across your face while you're scrubbing the kitchen with bleach, just push it back. No need to wash your hands before running your fingers through your hair; when you're done, you'll have this cool Bride-of-Frankenstein streak of white that's all the rage these days.

Household bleach has a divine counterpart, too; something that deep cleans, removes stains, purifies, and is far more precious and far more eternal! Churches still sing about this miracle all-purpose cleaner, in an old hymn:

> *What can wash away my sin?*
> *Nothing but the blood of Jesus.*
> *What can make me whole again?*
> *Nothing but the blood of Jesus.*
> *Oh, precious is the flow,*
> *That makes me white as snow.*

The blood of Jesus Christ has the power to cleanse us of all unrighteousness, remove the stain of any sin, purify (sanctify) the immortal spirit within each us. This is the blood that our Savior shed when he was crucified over 2000 years ago for our sins. "'Come now, let us settle the matter,' says the Lord. 'Though your sins are like scarlet, they shall be as white as snow; though they are red as crimson, they shall be like wool. If you are willing and obedient....'" (Isaiah 1:18 NIV)

But just like bleach, in order for this supernatural cleaning solution to work, it must first be applied. God applies the blood when we: acknowledge our sins and our need for a Savior; turn away from our sins (change the direction of our lives); trust Jesus for our salvation, and accept (by faith) His free gift of eternal life; and make Him the Lord of our lives.

"God is faithful and reliable. If we confess our sins, he forgives them and cleanses us from everything we've done wrong." (1 John 1:9 GWT)

Head of Steam

There's a neat little directorial trick first used in *Cat People*, a 1942 horror film produced by Val Lewton and directed by Jacques Tourneur. Despite its weird title, the movie is an intelligent and well done psychological study of ... *oh dear, we're starting to veer off on a tangent.* Anyway, in *Cat People*, there's a suspenseful nighttime sequence in which the movie heroine believes she's being stalked by something on a lonely New York sidewalk.

Cat People
(1942 RKO/ Warner Archive)

Just as the tension builds to the point viewers think they can't handle any more, something rushes into the scene with a loud hiss! After we toss our popcorn into the air, we realize it's just a city bus stopping to pick up passengers. This directorial technique came to be known as a "bus"—we hope you can guess why—and it's repeatedly used in movies to make us jump out of our skin. Anything that startles the viewer will work. Sometimes it's the unexpected ring of a phone piercing the silence, or the wail of a steam locomotive breaking the suspense.

Ever put the kettle on to boil and momentarily forget about it? We have. Once, while waiting to enjoy a cup of tea, we started washing and drying dishes ... and chatting; and yup, we forgot all about it. Meanwhile, the water in the kettle was getting hotter and hotter. Pressure built up in the vessel, and when it vented its steam, it suddenly shrieked at us! Not expecting a "bus" in the kitchen, we almost dropped a couple of plates! We weren't expecting the peace and quiet of our kitchen to be interrupted by a screaming kettle!

And that's the way we all feel when someone we know—possibly even care about—suddenly decides to vent in our direction. If the person is generally a peaceable soul, the sudden outburst can be totally unexpected, and it can hurt! If you've been the target of someone venting, a friend, coworker, or loved one, and you suffered a steam burn, you can learn the best way to handle such a situation, in the next chapter, "Cool It!" But for now, we'll discuss how to avoid spouting off at others in the first place.

We understand that sometimes the pressures of life build up in our tiny brains and overtaxed nervous systems, just like water coming to boil in a kettle. And if we've been holding it in, when we finally do vent, through some small outlet—perhaps a friend's normally sympathetic ear—our angst and anxiety erupts like a volcano! Angry words, negative comments, and loud tones spew out like scalding steam.

Physics lesson: why doesn't a saucepan scream at us when it lets off steam? Simple, it has a much larger opening through which to vent, so it's constantly allowing the heat to rise. And hence, there's no internal pressure building up. So, pots are peaceful? They can be, as we'll discuss later!

As people, we usually have one or two confidants to whom we vent. But, sometimes we bottle things up inside, refusing to talk about things that are bothering us, refusing to deal with issues that continue to build tension. Maybe there's a relationship that could benefit from more communication, a situation at work or church that needs to be addressed. Just talk. Don't wait till things are so bad that you blow up. Many times the person who hears us "shriek" isn't even the one who needs to hear what we have to say.

Are you a little hotheaded? You need to cool that down. There's an old expression concerning steam locomotives: "Build a head of steam." Tthis is good for trains because it helps them to move forward, but bad for people because it holds us back in just about every human endeavor. So how do we let off more steam more easily and more productively?

Like the saucepan, we need a larger opening, a larger direction to vent in. That would be God. Hey, He loves it when you vent. He longs to hear every little detail of every little problem you're facing. And letting off steam in His direction is much safer and far more productive. First, He always has the answers (which we find by reading His Word daily), and second, once you get it off your chest, you'll be much calmer when you get around the rest of us.

Good advice: Daily vent with the Lord, cool your head and calm your nerves with God's written promises, have the quiet time you need each and every day to avoid letting the cares of life build up inside you. You'll be doing less spouting off, less screaming—and less apologizing. Because, *yeah*, when you do unexpectedly and accidentally vent, you need to be just as quick to say you're sorry. We've all been there, we all understand about letting off steam, but we need to hear you say those comforting words: *I'm sorry.*

Okay? Now, how about that cup of tea?

"Let all that I am wait quietly before God, for my hope is

in him. He alone is my rock and my salvation, my fortress where I will not be shaken. My victory and honor come from God alone. He is my refuge, a rock where no enemy can reach me. O my people, trust in him at all times. Pour out your heart to him, for God is our refuge." (Psalm 62:5-8 NLT)

Cool It!

Steam burns can be bad. When steam hits flesh, it goes from a gaseous state back to a liquid state. This is a chemical change that releases energy in the form of more HEAT. That's why steam cleaning in so effective, and why steam burns are really bad. Steam releases heat that penetrates deep beneath the skin. And it can actually do damage under the surface. On top, the skin is inflamed, but often the wound is much deeper. That's why it's important to apply ice to a steam burn and cool the flesh quickly. Ice soothes, but more importantly, it also dissipates all that heat.

People tend to act like tea kettles. Just as the water in a kettle gets hotter and hotter, building up internal pressure until it finally vents its steam, people frequently allow the pressures of life to build until they can't handle any more —and they suddenly must vent! They erupt like a volcano, spouting scalding emotions and often caustic comments. Sooner or later we all have volcanic venting, but again, our more violent eruptions can be avoided by letting off steam with the Lord, a little each day.

Spend time reading God's Word and talk to the Lord about the pressures you're facing. God longs to hear every little detail of every little problem in our lives, and letting off steam in His direction is much safer and far more productive. He always has the answers and once we get things off our chests, we're calmer and better equipped to interact with others.

To avoid spouting off, daily vent with the Lord, cool your head and calm your nerves with God's written promises, have the quiet time you need each day to prevent the pressures of life from building up inside you. But what do you do when someone vents at you?

Yes, steam burns hurt, and the damage often penetrates deep! When people suddenly vent in our direction, the eruption of frustration and anger can be pretty scalding. Anger produces angry words. And misery really does like company, so hurting people often say hurtful things. It's important to remember not to take it personally when someone suddenly vents at you. No, you don't deserve such treatment—*who does?* But remember, the person has lost emotional control. He or she may say things they don't even mean to say, things they don't even believe to be true, but again, out of stress, frustration, anger, hate, fear, disappointment, jealousy—name your poison—the tongue can become a wicked and deadly weapon!

Try to avoid steam burns in the first place. Never shake a kettle when it's starting to boil inside. That's often the reverse of what people do. If they realize something's bothering someone, a coworker, for instance, they will frequently try to stir things up even further. Never poke a hornet's nest with a stick, no matter how long the stick or how fast you can run. Why would you, anyway?

If you're minding your own business and get caught in the blast of venting steam anyway, then please remember, *It's not personal!* These things happen. Treat an upset person the same way you'd want to be treated whenever you suddenly vent. And you eventually will. Do what you can to cool down the situation. "A gentle answer deflects anger, but harsh words make tempers flare." (Proverbs 15:1 NLT)

Sometimes there's absolutely nothing you can say, good or bad, that will help the situation. Sometimes distraught people don't want (or need) to hear your platitudes. In these situations, just keep your mouth shut and wait for the steam to dissipate. Keeping quiet may actually help the person cool off quicker.

Now, not "saying" anything also means that you refrain from communicating non-verbal messages using your face and body language. No smirking, no eye rolling, no Mister-Spock-eyebrow-lifting. Instead, be sympathetic. "Be happy with those who are happy, and weep with those who weep." (Romans 12:15 NLT)

Did you get a steam burn from someone you love, respect, or otherwise care about? Put some ice on it. Quickly, before the heat penetrates more deeply! Cool the hurt and soothe the pain by taking it to the Lord in prayer.

Come with your wounded spirit! Come with your broken heart! Whatever, then, be your present situation, seek the promised help of the Holy Spirit. He has a healing balm for all....
—John MacDuff (1818-1895)
The Throne of Grace

Cover It!

We goofed the other day, while cooking a couple of chili dinners. You're supposed to cut a slit in the plastic film covering these dinners and then microwave the trays for 90 seconds. We did that. Then you remove the plastic and stir. Did that too. Then the little black plastic trays go back in the microwave for another minute. We put one tray in "Luke" and the other in "Nuke," and then punched Quick Minute on our twin microwaves.

I'm LUKE! *He's* Nuke. Can't you see the difference between us?!

Luke and Nuke sang out *Beep!* almost in perfect harmony. We opened their doors and... What a mess! We've often heated dinners like these with no mishaps, but this time we forgot to put the plastic covers back on the trays. Guess we were busy talking about our book projects and absentmindedly tossed those protective plastic covers in the trash. Live and learn: It looked like something had exploded in these microwaves.

I'm NUKE! *He's* Luke. I'm better looking and more talented!

And that's pretty much what happened. Beans have a tendency to *POP!* when microwaved. When you have a bean explode, it hurls shrapnel in every direction: chili sauce, cheese, and bean fragments. The insides of Luke and Nuke were smeared with gunk!

Cleaning up this mess was time consuming and not much fun. But we knew we needed to fix our mess before the chili sauce and cheese dried and got hard. Believe it or not, we can all learn an incredible lesson from this unfortunate mishap. Yes, we all need to cover our dinners in the microwave, but we also need to frequently cover our mouths.

Words are like beans. When we get hot, they tend to *pop* out of our mouths and make an emotional mess! Ever have someone tell you to just speak your mind? Uh, we're not sure if we want to hear everything you're thinking. We have some friends whose mouths seem to work faster than their brains.

Forgive us for mixing our metaphors, but once the cow's out of the barn, it's too late to shut the barn door! So instead of blurting out things we may later regret, we need to carefully weigh our thoughts and words before they charge out of our mouths. Decide if what we're about to say is helpful. Will it improve the situation? Will it *build* the listener *up*, or *tear* the listener *down?*

We've all heard that "sticks and stones may break my bones, but words will never hurt me!" *Wrong!* "Death and life are in the power of the tongue." (Proverbs 18:21 KJB) Words have the ability to heal or to hurt. In fact, wars usually start and end with words. Words, when hurled by a malicious or unruly tongue, can wound like tiny spears.

Remember how as kids we'd embarrass our parents by blurting out some really stupid and inappropriate things? Maybe we even made fun of other kids. But hey, we were kids, right? Unfortunately, some of us still *are*, or at least we act like it. We take great pleasure in making smart comments, often at the expense of someone else's feelings. We gossip, insult, and aggravate with our words, never pausing to consider the damage we're doing.

The Apostle Paul writes, "When I was a child, I spoke and thought and reasoned as a child. But when I grew up, I put away childish things." (1 Corinthians 13:11 NLT)

In other words, stop spewing words that wound. This includes words that wound unintentionally—because some people seem to suffer from *Foot-In-Mouth Disease*. Whether, intentional or not, we can take precautions that will prevent making a mess, by covering the chili in the microwave and the words in our mouths. Cover those little black plastic trays with plastic; cover your mouths with prayer.

If you forget to cover your food before nuking it, you'll have a mess on the surfaces you can see and clean. But if you forget to cover your mouth, the mess you make is often unseen, smeared beneath the surface: hurt feelings, anger, and resentment. If you can't see these emotions, you can't clean the stains they leave. So they harden....

Ask God to cover your mouth: "Set a guard over my mouth, LORD; keep watch over the door of my lips."

(Psalm 141:3 NIV)

Put a Lid On It!

We just wrote about not covering a tray of food before nuking it, and the ugly mess we made in the microwave. We compared the incident to people not covering their mouths, and the mess they create by unthinkingly, or uncaringly speaking their minds. We'll further discuss the power of words, by telling you about "another nice mess" we made in the kitchen.

We had a large pot of stew cooking on the range. *Kabasi, potatoes, cabbage, onions.* We left the pot unattended for a few minutes, not expecting the contents to do much more than stew a little. (Heh!) We should have put a lid on it. When we returned, there was stew all over the range. *Kabasi, potatoes, cabbage, onions.* We worked a good 15 minutes cleaning up that mess. *Paper towels, Clorox, Brillo—sigh!*

Putting a lid on things can save a lot of time and aggravation. Things like arguments, for instance. (Yes, we're going to discuss this topic whether you like it or not! So don't argue with us!) Arguments can get messy, and the aftermath is hard to clean up. *Paper towels, Clorox, Brillo—sigh!*

"Well, here's another nice mess you've gotten me into."

Oliver Hardy and Stan Laurel in *You're Darn Tootin'* (1928 Hal Roach Studios)

It takes two to tango. It also takes two people to work up a good argument. Correct us if we're wrong, but no one ever got into an argument all by their lonesome. No, it takes two sets of opinions, two sets of emotions, two sets of tempers, and two sets of out-of-control attitudes. Bring together gas and a lit match and you'll have a little piece of Hell on earth. Take away either of these and things will remain fairly cool. Likewise, take away one set of anger and attitude, and *poof!*— no argument. So, why don't we?

Pride and emotion usually prevent us from putting a lid on things before they boil over. Left to our own devices, we demand to be heard, we demand to be right, we demand to retaliate, and we demand to have the last word! 30 years ago, not long after we were married, we attended Bill Gothard's *Institute in Basic Youth Conflicts*, and learned a Biblical Principle that has helped put a lid on many an argument before it really got started:

Surrender your right to be right. That's essentially what

Jesus did when he walked the earth. How can we not do the same? "...Have the same attitude that Christ Jesus had. Though he was God, he did not think of equality with God as something to cling to. Instead, he gave up his divine privileges [His rights]; ...He humbled himself in obedience to God...." (Philippians 2:5-8 NLT)

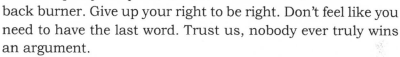

Adopting Christ's attitude can prevent or shorten most arguments; and curtail a lot of emotional turmoil. Humble your-self and put your pride on the back burner. Give up your right to be right. Don't feel like you need to have the last word. Trust us, nobody ever truly wins an argument.

What's more important? Peace, harmony and the preser-vation of a relationship, or hours, perhaps even days, of strife and discord—just so you can be right? "Love does not demand its own way. It is not irritable, and it keeps no record of being wronged." (1 Corinthians 13:5 NLT)

"Get rid of all bitterness, rage, anger, harsh words, and slander...." (Ephesians 4:31 NLT)

"...You must all be quick to listen, slow to speak, and slow to get angry." (James 1:19 NLT)

Don't get defensive. Don't be *argumentative!* Don't say things you'll later regret. Put a lid on your anger, pride, hurt. Try instead to defuse arguments with words of understand-ing: "A gentle answer deflects anger, but harsh words make tempers flare." (Proverbs 15:1 NLT)

You'll definitely need God's help in this. In fact, you can't do it without Him! So, pray like the Psalmist prayed: "Let the words of my mouth and the meditation of my heart be ac-ceptable in your sight, O LORD, my rock and my redeemer." (Psalm 19:14 ESV)

Fried with Words!

We don't often fry foods. Frying can be messy, and fried foods aren't very healthy. Once in a while, though, we do fry thin cut, lean pork chops. We set the gas at medium to control the heat and put a lid on the skillet to minimize the spatter of the sizzling olive oil. We previously discussed putting a lid on pots to prevent things from boiling over, and compared the precaution to "setting a guard" over our mouths, lest we blurt out stupid and hurtful words. Keeping a lid on things is the best way to avoid having to clean up a mess, whether it's on top of the gas range or in a relationship.

It's impossible, however, to keep a lid on the skillet throughout the entire frying process. You have to remove the lid to turn the chops (or whatever you're frying), and when you do, droplets of flesh-searing oil take the opportunity to spatter your hands and the top of the range. And—wouldn't you know it?—those red-hot spatters of grease are just like words!

Sooner or later, no matter how careful we are, we're going to say something stupid or hurtful. Furthermore, we're all sensitive about something, and some of us may be *overly* sensitive; so when we consider the human propensity for Foot-in-Mouth Disease, we realize that when interacting with others, eventually someone is bound to get burned by a sizzling word.

When frying food, we expect to have a few oil spatters, so we keep a sponge with a little ammonia nearby. When the skillet spats at us, we wipe away the grease right then and there. Cleaning things up fast is always best, because these spatters can be nasty and things can get sticky, just like harsh words in a relationship if not quickly dealt with. But what substitutes for ammonia when cleaning up the messes we make with our mouths? Something much stronger than ammonia, something that removes even the toughest stains. No, not Tide! *Love!*

We love old movies (and a few new ones, too), but movies, even the ones that seem realistic, are glamorized depictions of life. Hollywood tends to varnish life so it shines brighter. As though life weren't already bright enough—but then, that's why Hollywood is called Tinsel Town. It also espouses its own crazy philosophy. You can enjoy the show, without buying into everything Hollywood presents as "wisdom"! The 1970 tear-jerker *Love Story* is a great example: "Love means never having to say you're sorry." That might look good on a cheap tee-shirt, but if you practice this philosophy, you'll never have a "love story"—or any meaningful relationships!

True love is quick to say "I'm sorry"—wherever and whenever your words offend. And as often as your words offend! In fact, *true* love means actually getting into the habit of saying, "I'm sorry I hurt you again. I was wrong. Please forgive me." Here's the two-step cleaning process: first, apologize to God. "If we confess our sins, He is faithful and just to forgive us our sins and to cleanse us from all unrighteousness." (1 John 1:9 KJV)

Second, "Confess your faults one to another, and pray one for another, that you may be healed." (James 5:16 AKJ)

Making a habit of apologizing requires us to get rid of stinking pride. It's humbling to admit when we're wrong, but it's always necessary. And it takes God's grace, the supernatural strength to do what's right in a difficult situation. So take responsibility for your words and actions. Don't try to shift the blame. Don't make excuses for bad behavior.

Say the magic words: "I'm sorry." Say it like you mean it, and say it quickly, before the mess gets out of hand. Don't walk out the door or go to bed without making things right. Hurts build up and harden, like spattered grease on the range top. It's easier to clean it immediately than to wait for another time. Apologizing only gets harder the longer you wait.

> *...Don't let the sun go down while you are still angry.*
> —Ephesians 4:26 NLT

Mind the Language!

Hot *dogs* and *ham* burgers! Seriously? Of course not. There's no ham (or pork of any kind) in a hamburger. And you can eat a hotdog in front of your pet dachshund without feeling guilty. But these food names are just two examples of our crazy, sometimes confusing, English language. In the kitchen, in particular, our loony lingo truly takes the cake.

It turns out a pig in a blanket is perfectly kosher—as long as you're eating a Hebrew National frank. By the way, we're confused. What's the difference between a hotdog (also hot dog), a frankfurter and a wiener? Can we please reach a consensus on what to call these sausages? Why do hot dogs need a whole *pack* of names? Woof! Oh, and does the word *spicy* mean flavorful from spices, or simply HOT—a quality derived from the addition of peppers? There's no consensus on that one, either.

A Dutch oven isn't an oven at all. It's just a heavy, lidded pot—the kind you cook with, not what hippies and politicians used to smoke. French fries are not French; bread pudding is not the kind of pudding many think, it's a dense gelatinous mass of flour and raisins; A grilled cheese sandwich isn't really grilled; and is barbecue a cooking process, or a Southern dish of pulled pork?

What's up with eggplant? Did it grow from an egg? Maybe it's the offspring of chickweed. *Ouch!* Also, we hate for this to get out, but there's no egg in an egg cream drink. Do you love pizza? We do, too. We also love our friends, family, and our Lord. Wonder how God feels when we apply the same term of devotion to Him as we do to a slab of dough smeared with tomato sauce? In other languages—Spanish, for instance —there are separate verbs for differing types and levels of "love." Here, though, we can honestly say we love our spouse and the dog.

Adding to the confusion are regionalisms (expressions that developed in certain areas of the country) and slang. "He's a real piece of work" sounds good, but it ain't. "She's a space cadet" infers some stupidity, but wouldn't you need to be smart to go to Space Academy?

"Let's take a ride!" (No, we don't want to bump you off.) We'll *drive* in the *park*way, and when we get back, we'll *park* in the *drive*way. —Look out! We're about to run a stoplight! Or is it a "traffic light"? After all, it signals us to stop *and* go.

We've read that the English language is one of the most difficult "second" languages to learn, due to all its exceptions. Spelling? "I" before "E" except after "C"—but only on the third Wednesday of every other month. Does grammar sometimes prey on your mind? Maybe you should pray about it? What's the difference between "read" and "read"? Depends on whether you're starting a book or finishing it.

We could go on. But we simply want to emphasize that mastering the English language—and therefore, verbal communication—isn't a piece of cake. Nor is it as easy as pie. Sometimes we have trouble saying what we mean, and we don't always mean what we say. HELP!!!

God admonishes us to take care in what we speak, and in how we speak it. For instance: "Gentle words are a tree of life; a deceitful tongue crushes the spirit." (Proverbs 15:4 NLT)

Furthermore, research states that 80% of all communication is non-verbal. Our eyes, hands, and even our posture speak volumes. And we all know that "Actions speak louder than words." In fact, people pay more attention to what we *do* than to what we *say*. "Seeing is believing"! Application? Don't just *talk* about the teachings of Christ, MODEL them! Saint Francis of Assisi wrote, "Preach the Gospel at all times and when necessary use words."

"...Prove yourselves doers of the word, and not merely hearers who delude themselves." (James 1:22 NASB)

"...Speak my Word in truth...." (Jeremiah 23:28 NLT) In other words, *say* what you mean and *mean* what you say.

Scrambling Forward!

We once hosted some guests who quite inadvertently reminded us of an important lesson. Which we'll now pass on to you, dear reader. Because it's *eggs*-actly what we need.

One of our guests, when asked how she wanted her breakfast eggs, quickly responded scrambled. When she came downstairs to join her husband at the kitchen table, she found him about to enjoy two of the loveliest fried eggs you've ever seen. They were nestled between a couple slices of ham and a pile of hash browns. Contentedly occupying his plate like twin smiley faces. (Hey, we aim to please at Woodhaven.) His wife stared, as he eagerly cut through an egg and the warm yolk mingled with the ham and hash browns. Then she announced she wanted to cancel the scrambled eggs and have them fried instead.

One very big problem: her eggs had been cracked open, whisked together, and were in the process of being scrambled in a skillet with several pats of butter! *Too late*, we said, a little bewildered. These were the last two eggs in the house, they were now being scrambled, and you can't unscramble eggs. Period. You got scrambled eggs, lady. *Bon appétit!*

As with anything in life, we need to know what we want, understand what's involved, make better plans, and be careful not to break any yolks. Meanwhile, all is not lost. Scrambled eggs are great, especially with crispy bacon and toast!

Sometimes we get scrambled eggs in life. We make mistakes. We make the wrong decisions. We break our promises and get our priorities scrambled. We make a jumble of our relationships. But we can't unscramble the messes we make. Certain situations in our lives may no longer be appealing, but we can't rewrite history. We can't reclaim the rich, golden yolks of opportunities missed, or repair a fragile relationship once it's cracked apart. What we can do is to live and learn: *Live* to our utmost potential, with God's infinite love and strong support: and when we *do* fail (and we *will*, repeatedly), then *Learn* from our failings.

We all have regrets. If we had time machines, many of us would spend so much time in the past, trying to fix things, that we'd miss out on what the future holds. The Apostle Paul once wrote: "I don't mean to say that... I have already reached perfection. ...No, dear brothers and sisters, I have not achieved it, but I focus on this one thing: Forgetting the past and looking forward to what lies ahead, I press on...." (Philippians 3:12-13 NLT)

We can't unscramble our past mistakes. So learn the lessons they teach, but put the mistakes behind you. And then move forward. Everyday provides new opportunities.

Yolks and Folks!

We just compared past mistakes and failures to scrambled eggs, reminding you that what's done can't be undone—so you need to forget the past and focus on the future. To ensure you don't get bored with what we're serving up in *Angel in the Kitchen*, we've decided to move on to a totally new topic offering fresh insights. We're done with *scrambled* eggs. We'll now discuss omelets! How's that for being different? (Hey, our humor can be *eggs-quisitely* painful.)

What can the omelet teach us? Before we dish out that info, let's first learn some cool facts about eggs. (Trust us, we're not stalling. This will all tie in later.)

Eggs are a very versatile food: they can be boiled, poached, pickled, fried, scrambled, deviled, made into omelets, blended into shakes, or added to cakes, pies, puddings and soufflés. And if you're Rocky Balboa, you can crack six of them into a tumbler and drink 'em down raw before you go out to jog the streets of Philly. ("Yo, Adrian, I did it!")

There are many types of eggs used in recipes, the most popular being hen eggs. There are around eight varieties of hen eggs. Other types include quail eggs, ostrich eggs, emu eggs, duck eggs, and Guinea Fowl eggs. There are different colors, too. Hen eggs can be white, speckled, or range from buff to light golden brown to a dark reddish brown. There's even a green-tinted egg, the Ameraucana.

Eggs also come in different sizes. An average size Ostrich egg is about 13 centimeters (or 6 inches) and weighs roughly 3 pounds. One of these babies is equal to 12 extra-large hen eggs, so you could feed breakfast to a family of four using a single egg. Of course, Ostrich eggs may be hazardous to your health; ostriches are good parents, and they can run over 40 mph! Oh, and they have really big feet to stomp you with!

The smallest bird egg comes from the bee hummingbird, and averages about a quarter-inch. Not much food in these, but come on, who wants to deprive the world of another cute little hummingbird?

For the purpose of making a point, we'll stick to hen eggs in the preparation of our omelet today. Inter-estingly, despite the dif-ference in the color of their shells, which do nothing more than indicate the type of hen they came from, all hen eggs are pretty much the same. Inside, their yolks are yellow, and they have the same nutritional value. Lots of info, but what's our point? A very simple one, which we hope to re-inforce by sharing all these cool facts. Namely, people are like eggs. We come in all sizes and colors. We come from different ethnic groups and nationalities, just as cooking eggs come from many different types of fowl. Yet we are all equal.

And what's truly amazing about eggs *and* people? If you have a mind to—and we repeat—if you have a mind to, you can blend the many differing types and colors into a single delicious "omelet." Once you do, you won't be able to dis-tinguish which eggs were used. Looks like an omelet. Tastes like an omelet. Hey, it *is* an omelet!

God desires all of humankind to blend together in the same way. We're all the same inside, so why can't we join together? We may have slightly different flavors (strengths, gifts, abilities, backgrounds and experiences), but those dif-fering flavors can blend beautifully in an omelet (family or congregation, organization or community). Throw in some Holy Spirit seasoning, and we'll have one incredibly palatable world.

"There is neither Jew nor Gentile, neither slave nor free,

nor is there male and female, for you are all one in Christ Jesus." (Galatians 3:28 NIV)

How to Ruin a Good Omelet!

Ever hear someone say, "He's a good egg"?

We've been discussing how similar people are to eggs, and a few of our readers probably think we've finally cracked. *Ouch!* Eggs, like people, come in different sizes and colors. Eggs, like people, can have different backgrounds: eggs can be from hens, ducks, quails, emus, ostriches, etc.; and people can be from different ethnic groups or countries, have different gifts, talents, life experiences, etc. But despite all the differences, eggs and people are pretty much the same inside. Yolks and Folks are all equal once you get to know them, once you penetrate their shells.

Eggs, regardless of origin, color, or size, can blend perfectly together in an omelet. Similarly, people can blend to create a harmonious family, neighborhood, faith community or work environment.

There is, however, one egg you never want in your omelet, because it can spoil the whole dish: a *rotten* egg! We learned the hard way. Whisk together a single rotten egg in a dish with eleven good eggs, and you get an egg mixture that stinks! One rotten egg manages to contaminate all the other eggs. Which is why we "screen" our eggs. It's easier to simply crack all the eggs into a single bowl when cooking, but we advise against it. Once the rotten egg is in the mix, it's impossible to separate it. So we crack each egg into a small dish, examine it and smell it, before adding it to whatever we're preparing.

Bet you're way ahead us this time. Yes, the same goes for people. One rotten egg can spoil your workplace, your club, your house of worship, and even your home!

So what makes a rotten egg? How about attitude? If you pay close attention, you can see the effect that a negative person can have on the moral of those around them. People within any type of group can be enthusiastic, ready to try new ideas and get the job done, but add one negative attitude, one person whose motto is "It can't be done"; whose mantra is "It will never work"; someone who truly delights in raining on other people's parades; and pretty soon everyone's morale starts to drop. Say goodbye to a winning team, say hello to an "omelet" that stinks through and through!

Remember the twelve spies who reconnoitered the Promised Land? (You can read the story in Numbers 13.) Two returned with positive attitudes: "We can defeat the Giants and claim the promise!" But there were ten rotten eggs in the dozen. They said, "We won't succeed," and their stinking attitudes soon permeated the entire camp of the Hebrews, contaminating enough of the people that "The LORD was not able to bring these people into the land he promised them...." (Numbers 14:16 NIV)

Sometimes people speak words of gloom and doom simply because they themselves have repeatedly suffered defeat and have lost faith. But there are many other reasons people have stinking thinking. They may be fearful. They may just like to argue. They may be jealous or mean-spirited. They may suffer from feelings of inferiority and feel the need to build themselves *up* by putting others *down*. Whatever the cause, their rottenness can manifest itself in other ways, none of them healthy to the "omelet":

Put-down humor, making fun of others, or telling jokes at someone's expense! Nobody enjoys this type of humor when they're the target. "Throw out the mocker, and fighting goes, too; Quarrels and insults will disappear." (Proverbs 22:10 NLT)

Vulgarity and perverseness in the form of crude jokes, foul language, or sexual references. "Do not let any unwholesome talk come out of your mouths, but only what is helpful for building others up according to their needs, that it may benefit those who listen." (Ephesians 4:29 NIV)

A critical or judgmental spirit. "Brothers and sisters, stop complaining about each other, or you will be condemned. Realize that the judge is standing at the door." (James 5:9 GWT)

How about gossip? The goal of a gossiper is usually to slander someone, but regardless of the motive, gossip is always divisive! A gossiper can destroy loyalties and relationships, disrupting the harmony within any group. "A perverse person stirs up conflict, and a gossip separates close friends." (Proverbs 16:28 NIV)

And how about rotten Integrity? That kills trust in any group. So, "Whoever lives honestly will live securely, but whoever lives dishonestly will be found out." (Proverbs 10:9 GWT)

If you don't want your "omelet" to stink, you'll need to get rid of the rotten eggs. In cooking, we toss them into the garbage disposal. But we don't throw away people with rotten attitudes. *Never!* We first try to help them. We admonish them. And we love them. But if they refuse to change, we'll need to follow Pastor Joel Osteen's advice and "Love them from a distance." We can still be friendly and continue to help when we can, but we won't be able to enter into any form of "partnership" with them.

Rotten eggs can make you sick! So please try to be a good egg! "Speech that heals is like a life-giving tree, but a perverse tongue breaks the spirit." (Proverbs 15:4 NET Bible)

Microwave Mentality

We love our twin microwaves Luke and Nuke. They're such a blessing that it's hard not to get attached to them. They're essential members of our family of kitchen appliances, and now we can't imagine life without them. We can actually pop *two* bags of popcorn at the same time! Does it get any better than that?

Microwaves make life a lot easier. And they speed up many kitchen tasks. A baked potato used to take over an hour in a conventional oven. A microwave gets the job done in a few minutes. Frozen dinners, originally packaged in foil trays and engineered to be heated in the oven, went from taking at least half an hour to "cook," to being ready in a couple minutes.

The microwave oven was "invented" in 1945 by Raytheon. One of their employees, Percy Spencer, a self-taught engineer from Maine, had discovered the microwave's ability to heat foods by sheer accident. He was working on a radar system, when he noticed the microwaves being emitted were melting the chocolate bar he'd stuck in his pocket. Leave it to a scientist to react positively to such a revelation: "Wow, that is so cool!" versus "Yikes, my goose could've been cooked!"

Spencer quickly cobbled together a microwave device to try cooking other foods. First thing he microwaved was—*surprise!*—Popcorn. (Orville Redenbacher really owes this guy.) The second thing was an egg, which—*surprise!*—exploded in the face of one of his technicians. Two years later, Raytheon filed a U.S. patent application for Spencer's gift to humankind and started manufacturing the first commercially available microwave ovens. Speedy Weeny purchased one and installed it in a vending machine in New York's Grand Central Station, allowing passengers to dispense "sizzling delicious" hot dogs in little more than a minute.

It was two decades before microwave ovens were made available for home use. Raytheon's first commercially available microwave was almost 6 feet tall, weighed in at 750 pounds, and cost about $5,000—close to $53,000 in today's U.S. dollars—a mere pittance. But in 1967, Amana introduced the first kitchen countertop model. New technology and innovation allowed microwave ovens to be built lighter, smaller and less expensive.

Isn't technology wonderful? *No, we really mean it.* Technological advances are the reason computers went from filling up huge buildings and costing millions, to fitting in our cell phones—and being relatively cheap. Innovation has given us fast food, and then speeded up the process of take-out meals even further by giving us the drive-thru.

After taking a snapshot, we used to have to wait for days before we could see the results of the developed film. Then someone created the one-hour photo shop. But even that seems slow by today's standards: now we just capture images with our phones and we can see the pics immediately. Life is good, right? It's also really fast. High-speed internet, express checkout, instant oatmeal, and Jiffy Lube! Fast and convenient. But with all these time-saving innovations, many of us have gotten a "microwave mentality": we want everything now! And that's only because we can't have it "yesterday"!

We're living in fast times. We have accelerated lifestyles. We want to accomplish more in less time. This can be an admirable quality ... until it becomes an obsession. Being in a constant hurry can be taxing to your nervous system. People get impatient when they have to wait—even if it's only a few minutes. When they get off from

But I want it now!

work, they start the mad dash to get home, which is why we call this time of day *The Rush Hour!* But haste makes waste: fender benders take time to phone in and get repaired; speeding tickets are expensive, and police officers usually write them up at a leisurely pace—maybe these officers are trying to impart a valuable lesson to motorists, and people in general: Slow Down!

We'd like to remind our readers to take life a little more slowly. Don't be in such a frenzy to get this, do that, or arrive there. Enjoy the journey. Take in the view. Stop and smell the roses. Calm down and sense the presence of the Lord. "Be still and know that I am God!" (Psalm 46:10 NLT)

Do You Do Stew?

What's cookin'? A stew! Stews (and stewing) are as old as cooking. A Roman cookbook published during the 4th century AD mentions stew; but most of us know of an even earlier reference to the dish, in the Biblical book of Genesis, which historians believe was written between 1410 and 1450 BC. As recorded in Genesis 25:27-34, an apparently extremely hungry Esau—who also was apparently extremely short-sighted—sold his Jewish birthright to his younger brother, Jacob—for a bowl of meat and lentil stew.

Esau thereby gave up pretty much everything that counted in his culture, but hey, can we really blame him?

After all, we're talking about STEW here: a tender, savory mixture of meat, fish, or poultry, and assorted vegetables—cooked with a little water for an extended period over a low heat. Stewing foods means that the cook brings them to a slow boil, and then allows them to simmer. Meats and veggies stew in their own juices, allowing the flavors to truly blend and seep in. Meats are suffused with the aromatic flavors of spices and fresh veggies, such as onions, peas and carrots. Hungry yet? Well don't forget that rich brown gravy that envelopes most stews! *Mmmm!*

There's another definition of the verb *stew*: to worry, to sulk or to fuss. And as with the culinary definition, performing this "action" will yield similar results: a stew! In this sense, a stew means a state of agitation, uneasiness, or worry. Interestingly, the emotional "cooking" process is pretty much the same. A mixture of different, and often conflicting, thoughts and feelings fill our minds, and we allow these thoughts to simmer. For an extended period. Over a low heat, as our emotions come to a boil. The results of our stewing are that feelings of fear, hurt, doubt, and anger blend together and seep in—deeply! The results, however, are far from pleasing.

We're all familiar with the idiom "to stew in one's own juice"; but when we do this, negative thoughts and emotions penetrate deeper and deeper, the way spices penetrate and suffuse stewed beef. Hurts, when allowed to simmer in our hearts, can suffuse our attitude toward every situation and every person.

Anger, after a long period of stewing, can lead to bitterness and an inability to forgive. When we allow worry to simmer in our thoughts, we eventually become nervous wrecks. And fear? Allow fear to simmer very long with your other emotions, and soon its horrid flavor will taint your entire outlook on life. In any of these scenarios, we're essentially "cooking" our own hearts and minds, only this emotional stew doesn't produce tender results.

God doesn't want us stewing over stuff. That's why he admonishes us to take several important steps. For instance, are you mad about something? Are you upset with someone? "Don't sin by letting anger control you. Don't let the sun go down while you are still angry." (Ephesians 4:26 NLT) Meaning: resolve your issues and/or turn the situation over to God, trusting Him to heal your hurts. In other words, get over it before the day is done, so that you can move forward.

Are you facing big problems or issues that have you worried? "Don't worry about anything; instead, pray about everything. Tell God what you need and thank him for all he has done." (Philippians 4:6 NLT) Hey, this verse says it all. Besides, worrying accomplishes nothing but a sour stomach.

Fearful?

"Don't be afraid, for I am with you. Don't be discouraged, for I am your God. I will strengthen you and help you. I will hold you up with my victorious right hand." (Isaiah 41:10 NLT) "For God has not given us a spirit of fear and timidity, but of power, love, and self-discipline." (2 Timothy 1:7 NLT)

Has someone hurt you?

"Bless those who persecute you. Don't curse them; pray that God will bless them." (Roman 12:14 NLT) Stop stewing, before all the wrong juices seep into your soul. "Watch out that no poisonous root of bitterness grows up to trouble you, corrupting many." (Hebrews 12:15 NLT)

Pop Culture

Why do some people make friends more easily than others? For that matter, why are some people more likable than others? Tough questions. Before we discuss these issues, let's take a break and pop the top on an ice-cold can of soda.

Did you know that Coca Cola goes all the back to 1886? Like a lot of sodas, Coke was initially sold in drug stores, because at the time, people strongly believed that carbonated water was beneficial to health. We doubt many nutritionists would agree with this today, but carbonation does have some soothing qualities. Besides being thoroughly refreshing, a cold Ginger ale can calm an upset stomach.

An icy bottle of Pepsi on a hot summer's day is sublime. Mountain Dew is a great pick-me-up and is extremely popular these days; but when we were kids, nothing could beat a Coke! "Things go better with Coke"—even if this *is* the "Pepsi Generation"! But actually, we now drink Diet Rite when we want a soda. We also drink lots of water. Every calorie counts, you know.

All these drinks have one thing in common. They're bubbly. Effervescent. Fizzy. Most people enjoy bubbly drinks. The fizz adds *pizzazz*. One thing's for sure, when the fizz is gone, the soda is far less palatable. And when cola goes flat... *yuck*, it's worse than Kool-Ade. We'd rather do without than drink a flat soda. A can of pop with no *pop* has far less to offer. Again, those little bubbles tickle our senses. We love the effervescence!

People are like cola. When they've lost their effervescence —their enthusiasm, their excitement toward life—when their personality and outlook on the world go flat, they're far less tolerable. Most of us love to hang out with bubbly people, so bubbly people make friends more easily. They have a sparkling personality that comes from a positive attitude and a contagious enthusiasm. Such people become very *POPular!* When we're around them, we feel encouraged, uplifted, and invigorated.

On the other hand, the bad attitudes and sour dispositions of people who've gone "flat" can be hard to swallow. No one enjoys being around a negative or bitter person. Why would we? Do you have a "woe is me" family member with the ability to rain on your every parade? Have you ever dealt with a coworker who knew any given project was "doomed to failure" before it even got started? Have you ever visited an "all gloom and doom" friend, and afterwards felt like you were ready to commit suicide? "Flat" friends and family are no fun. Their fizz is all gone. All that's left is the nasty Kool-Ade of their bleak outlook on life—and who wants to drink that?

What's our point? We need to try and be tolerant of these folk. We often can help lift their spirits. Inject some fizz back into lives. *But* we don't want to *be* these folks! We want to be POPular (in a good way), bubbly, encouraging, uplifting, crisp, cool and sparkling! Besides being friendly, *that's* how you really attract people and make friends. But getting back your fizz requires certain steps; and keeping your effervescence requires certain precautions.

You can't constantly fill your head with negative, pessimistic, gloomy, downer thoughts and ideas if you want to stay bubbly and be a part of the "Pop Culture." Ever watch a depressing movie and walk out of the theater all depressed? Hey, we're not asking you to never watch a tear-jerker, or to avoid people with nasty attitudes; but you need to make sure you pour into your life *more* good stuff than bad. Here's what the Apostle Paul has to say about it: "And now, dear brothers and sisters, one final thing. Fix your thoughts on what is true, and honorable, and right, and pure, and lovely, and admirable. Think about things that are excellent and worthy of praise." (Philippians 4:8 NLT)

Make Life Sweet!

Hey, sugar! No, not you! We certainly hope you're a sweet person, but today we're referring to that granulated stuff on the kitchen counter: table sugar; brown sugar, confectioners' sugar ... *shoog-er!* ("Ahhhh, honey, honey!") Sugar is one of those things that make life more enjoyable. If you've had a hard day, there's nothing quite like something sweet to bring a little cheer. And sugar manages to find itself in a variety of foods, including items you'd never suspect, such as canned green beans!

Sugar dates back to ancient times, but because it wasn't always plentiful or affordable, most people sweetened with honey, instead. But now sugar is everywhere. In fact, the world produces over 200 million metric tons of sugar each year. And the average person consumes about 53 pounds (or 24 kilograms) of it annually. Face it, we prefer things in life to be sweet.

One morning we were about to have our extra-dark coffee, along with our daily time of praise and worship, and we got an eye-opening revelation: we forgot the sugar! We both took one sip of the brew and then made faces at each other. It was bitter as quinine! Not that either of us has ever tasted quinine, mind you, but it is a familiar expression. How can something so tasty *with* sugar be so horrible *without* it? Now, we know some of you probably do like it black, but we prefer a teaspoon of sugar. Or honey. Or Splenda. Or Stevia. Or *something* sweet!

There's a lot of truth to the song actress Julie Andrews sang in Walt Disney's *Mary Poppins*: "Just a spoonful of sugar makes the medicine go down!" And ya know what? Love is the spiritual sugar of life! A little love can help us swallow even the often bitter pills of everyday existence. This is important to remember. If you've ever had to confront someone with the truth, then you probably know this.

The unvarnished truth can be painful. Truth forces us to face facts ... about ourselves and our choices. *Truth*—in essence, the Word of God—is like a brightly lit mirror that exposes all our flaws. And a little reassurance in the form of love makes facing the truth much easier to handle! That's why the Bible commands us to "speak the truth in love." (Ephesians 4:15)

Part of speaking the truth is sharing the Good News of salvation through Jesus Christ. By all means, do this in love. After all, God is Love (1 John 4:7), and salvation is about His love for us. (John 3:16) We need to be able to communicate this love in our attitudes and actions, as well as in our words. As a matter of fact, everything we do—whether correcting a child or discussing a problem (or a controversial issue) with a spouse, friend, or coworker—should always be done in love. No matter how right you are, no matter how justified your actions, if you fail to respond in love, then you lose the "high ground"! Hence, there's a good chance you'll lose the "argument"—so to speak.

If you confront someone with the truth, but do it in anger, that person will mostly see only your anger. You may be right, but you get no points because you lost control. And if the other guy stays calm, guess who looks "wrong" in this situation? Of course, we should never approach sharing truth as an opportunity to be right. Getting out the truth isn't about "Aha, I'm right and you're wrong!" That's *Pride!* God wants us to share the truth in LOVE—not pride. "Be completely humble and gentle; be patient, bearing with one another in love." (Ephesians 4:2 NIV)

So, walk in love—and humility. As the old saying goes: "You can attract more bees with honey than with vinegar." Love will win people over, not anger or arrogance. Be a sweet soul, not a bitter or sour one. Get God's sugar—*er*, love—in your heart and life.

> *...Above all things have fervent love among yourselves:*
> *for love covers a multitude of sins.*
> —1 Peter 4:8 KJ2000

The Perfect Food

Honey is often called "the perfect food." We agree that it's a natural food, created by cute lil' honeybees, and it's a healthier sweetener than processed sugar; however, it's far from perfect. If it were perfect, it wouldn't be fattening or promote tooth decay. Yes, we probably sound like a couple of grinches, but we want to make a valid point: there are no perfect foods!

Every food and every dish has a downside that can be a bummer if we allow it. At the core of that delicious apple a day is a seed-filled fibrous mass that's not very appetizing. Oranges have thick peels, string beans are... *uh*, stringy! Succulent crab legs have shells hard enough to crack your knuckles.

Those absolutely divine Mocha MooLattes from DQ can induce a severe brain freeze that'll make your eyeballs pop out; and eating pistachios causes sore thumbnails! (We'll leave you to figure out that one for yourselves.) And if there's a food that's light, airy, soft and sinfully sweet, such as cinnamon rolls, it's also bad for your heart, arteries, and waistline. Yes, we need to exercise self-control, eat certain foods in moderation, and deal with the downside of various nutritional items. But indeed, upon closer scrutiny and analysis, there are definite drawbacks to everything we consume. (Did you know you can drink too much water? Too much water can

flood tissues and flush out beneficial electrolytes.)

Now, most of us don't go through life begrudging meals because they're imperfect. We're not constantly *dissing* fruit because we have to peel it, or cursing Little Debbie because those Swiss Cake Rolls are hardening our arteries. No, we understand there are a few cons to go along with all the pros; we know that food is delicious and nutritious, and rarely think of it as being imperfect—and yet, it is. *No food is perfect.*

Life is like food: nothing in life is perfect, not the weather, your job, your boss, or the commute to work; not your spouse, your friend, your child, or your pastor. Face it, on this great big blue marble we call earth, there's very little perfection, because none of us—allow us to reiterate—not a single one of us, is perfect. It's a simple fact of life. What's important is how we view and handle our imperfect jobs, friends, family, etc. Do we get all bent out of shape over fruit that's nutritious but has to be peeled and pitted? Do we get disgusted with foods that are delicious but fattening? No, we generally take the good while overlooking the bad. And we adjust our expectations.

By now, someone's got to be thinking, "Yeah, but I expect more from life and people than I do from food!" And therein lies the problem: life and people are not perfect, but we often expect them to be! Unfortunately, when our expectations are too high, we're in for one huge disappointment after another. Sooner or later, your friends and family, your pastor or your boss will let you down. It's one of the cold hard facts of life. And the greater your expectations, the greater your disappointment will be.

So, what's the solution?

First: Keep your lofty expectations and always hope for the best—*but don't put your expectations on people.*

Instead, put your expectations on God. HE is perfect, and He'll never disappoint you. When you focus on HIS perfection, HIS faithfulness, HIS love, HIS care, HIS provision ... everything else in life, no matter how imperfect, suddenly becomes a lot more palatable. (See "Spit the Seeds!")

> *Upon God alone, O my soul, rest peacefully;*
> *for my expectation is from him.*
> —Psalm 62:5 Darby Bible

Junk Food

When it comes to food, do you have certain "guilty pleasures" you love to indulge in? It's okay, we all do. We could eat New York-style pizza every single day. But that would be extreme carbo-loading, and since we're not planning to run any marathons in the near future, we probably shouldn't. We're also fans of Edy's Ice Cream, specifically Cherry Chocolate Chip! *It. Is. Divine!*

Crunch 'n Munch? You know, caramel and chocolate drenched popcorn and peanuts? We also recall another brand, Moose Munch, which is an odd bit of nomenclature for a snack ... unless you happen to be one of those huge high school football players whose name really *is* "Moose"!

Cinnamon rolls. Anybody's! It doesn't matter, although Cinnabon—to quote a line from Ben Stiller's movie *The Secret Life of Walter Mitty*—"That's frosted heroin"! And don't get us started on Tiramisu! Please, because sometimes we need serious help. Chocolate eclairs, Lay's Mesquite Barbecue Potato Chips, and those little donuts that are dusted with a suspicious-looking white powder!!! No, we're not paid to advertise, although the companies whose junk food we're listing here ... they really should reward us by sending us a year's supply of everything.

Statistics show that people consume tons of junk food. Bags, boxes, buckets, and barrels full. Why do we love it so much? A couple reasons: First, it's either very sweet or very salty, very crunchy or very smooth and creamy. These qualities especially appeal to the palate. Second, for many of us, these snacks are our comfort food. After a hard day of work or school, we want to reward ourselves with something sinfully delicious. It's an old movie cliché, when someone is upset or depressed, they drown their sorrows with a pint of Ben & Jerry's. Of course, the morning after some such binge, massive guilt sets in.

Junk food is great—occasionally—but it needs to be balanced out with more nutritional fare. A diet of nothing but comfort foods can lead to serious health issues, such as high cholesterol and diabetes. So let the "consumer" be aware.

There are other types of "junk food": things we take comfort in; activities we tend to overindulge in; "stuff" we use to escape the pressures of life. Television, movies, sports, video games, graphic novels, magazines, the internet and—what's your poison? We love these things and activities because, like junk food, they greatly appeal to our appetites. And although such things, just like chips and candy, are not bad for us in moderation, when we binge on them, when we "diet" exclusively on such things, our brains and our spirits can get sick! We need fresh air and sunshine and healthy "spiritual food" to balance out the lighter and—we hope, only occasional—junky snacking we all tend to indulge in. We need to "consume" some of God's Word, the "Bread of Life," each day. (Matthew 4:4)

We can continue to escape with "comfort foods," but we need to remember that it is just an escape; and like snacks that provide nothing but empty calories and no real nourishment, we'll still be hungry for something more. "The true bread of God is the one who comes down from heaven and gives life to the world. ...I am the Bread of Life. Whoever comes to me will never be hungry again." (John 6:33, 35 NLT)

Are you continually putting more "sugar and fat" into your system than you are "vitamins and protein"? You've often heard the quote, "You are what you eat"?

Are you made of junk food? Are you glued to the boob tube? Is your ear stuck to the telephone? Have your fingers meshed with the keyboard? "As [a person] thinks in his heart, so he is." (Proverbs 23:7)

In other words, what we feed our minds shapes who we are. Everything we watch, read, hear, and speak out, affects our outlook on life, as well as our general disposition. Truly, the *way* we think, and *what* we think, makes each of who we are. Filling our heads with junk that's *hateful, critical, violent and vulgar* will ultimately make us people who are *hateful, critical, violent and vulgar.*

Yes, too much junk food can be hazardous to the spirit, soul and body. So, make sure you're consuming plenty of healthy brain food. "Fix your thoughts on what is true, and honorable, and right, and pure, and lovely, and admirable. Think about things that are excellent and worthy of praise." (Philippians 4:8 NLT)

Processed Food

Now that we've discussed those gastronomic guilty pleasures we all indulge in—junk food—and how a diet consisting mainly of these sugary, starchy and fatty treats is bad for our health. Similarly, there are "junk food" activities people tend to over-indulge in: television, movies, sports, video games, graphic novels, magazines, the internet, etc.; and a lifestyle consisting mainly of such activities is bad for our spiritual health. We stressed the need to get some fresh air and sunshine and, and in particular, to "consume" some of God's Word each day, the "Bread of Life"!

In the kitchen: most people believe enjoying a "healthy" diet is as simple as opening a can of soup. A bowl of soup is better than a bowl of ice cream, but is it—as an example of good nutrition—our *best* option? Hardly. Most canned soups and vegetables contain lots of additives we don't need in our systems. Some canned goods contain enormous amounts of sodium, the repeated consumption of which can lead to high blood pressure. Health experts warn us to limit these processed foods the same way we should limit junk food.

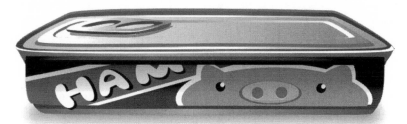

SIGH!! There's just no substitute for fresh, natural, unprocessed fruits, veggies, grains and nuts: the foods God created—only not tampered with!

Now, this is not to say there's no nutritional value in processed foods. For instance, a glass of supermarket orange juice is loaded with Vitamin C. How do we know? It says so, right on the carton: "Fortified with Vitamin C"! *But wait a minute.* Have you ever wondered why the juice from oranges— one of God's best sources of Vitamin C—needs to be "fortified" with synthetic Vitamin C (in other words, have more added)? Simple answer, really.

When oranges are cut and squeezed, a good deal of the Vitamin C oxidizes—it "dies"! (This natural oxidation is the same reason a sliced apple starts to turn brown after a few minutes.) Supermarket orange juice is also "processed" to extend the shelflife, further destroying the natural Vitamin content. But not to worry, to replace what's been lost, the factory has added some Vitamin C that was created in a lab. (Sounds like something from a 1950s sci-fi movie!)

Other common "additives" (a euphemism for chemicals) in processed foods include preservatives and dyes, all of which can have an effect on our health. Of course, this is again assuming we eat nothing but processed foods. We *don't* personally, but we sometimes do enjoy a serving of canned sweet corn, a bowl of cereal, a glass of bottled cranberry juice ... but we're careful to consume plenty of fresh fruit and veggies, too. *Balance is key!*

Spiritual application: We're blessed to have access to a wide variety of spiritually uplifting materials. Christian TV, radio, devotionals, and praise music. All of these resources draw inspiration (we hope) from the Word of God; but these wonderful Christian resources are, by their very nature, "processed" spiritual food. Sermons, praise CDs, Sunday school lessons, and hours spent watching inspirational shows, are all intended to be teaching aides and further sources of encouragement. But they should never replace personal daily Bible reading.

These spiritual supplements contain elements of God's Word, and the Word of God is *never* wasted. It always has impact. (Isaiah 55:11) But these are not pure and unadulterated sources of God's Word. In praise music, the Word has been slightly diluted; in an inspirational message, the speaker tends to toss in a few additives. Yes, make good use of all these resources. They come in handy in a pinch, and they help round out a "heart-healthy" meal; but do remember to balance out your spiritual diet by daily devouring large portions of the Word of God, the FRESH, 100% PURE, ALL NATURAL, WITH NOTHING ADDED "Bread of Life"!

...Long for the pure milk of the Word, so that by it
you may grow in respect to salvation....
—1 Peter 2:2 NASB

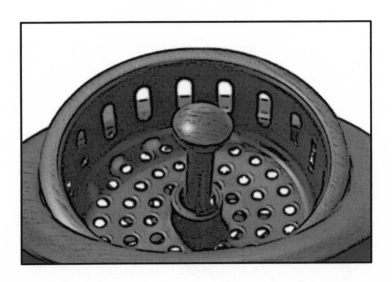

Preventing Clogs

Here's a trivia question for you: What do you call the funny little metal cup that fits in the drain of the kitchen sink and works like a mini colander? Is it called a strainer basket? We've also heard it called drainer basket, sink basket, basket drainer, or that "funny little metal cup that fits in the drain of the kitchen sink"! Whatever it's called, thank God it's there because it really works well to prevent a lot of problems.

Whoever came up with the idea should have gotten a medal, and maybe he or she did. Then again, the basket drainer should have been a no-brainer. (Did you read how that rhymed?) At some point, someone must have realized that all kinds of stuff was going down the drain and clogging the pipes. Maybe in the beginning someone simply put a piece of cloth, or even a section of metal screen, over the drain to keep chunks of food from going down the pipes.

You'd be amazed at the innovations people come up with in order to avoid trouble on down the line (pardon the pun) and, hence, extra work. Who wants a clogged pipe? The water backs up and the sink becomes useless. And anyone with an ounce of foresight can look at that huge drain opening and imagine everything from broccoli stumps to chicken bones going down the pipe. Well, almost anyone; we wonder if Drano was invented by someone with no foresight?

Believe it or not, God gave each of us enough foresight to know that there are certain preventive measures we need to take. God has given each of us the equivalent of a strainer basket, and He expects us to use it.

The Holy Spirit acts as a strainer basket. He "guides us into all truths" (John 16:13) and thereby enables us to determine right from wrong; and thus to make wise decisions. So we're not "swallowing" everything that comes down the social pipeline. We're not swallowing the half-truths and out-right lies we hear daily, or the false teachings of strange religions.

We're living in an age that preaches relativism: "right" and "wrong" frequently change depending on circumstances or the needs and desires of the social majority; and there are "grey areas." Not true! There are absolutes in life, based on the Word of God, which allow us to determine right from wrong. These absolutes (call them "standards") provide reference points for the moral compass everyone needs to stay on target. Without the absolutes and standards set by God's Word, we can easily lose our way and get lost.

"You are truly my disciples if you remain faithful to my teachings. And you will know the truth, and the truth will set you free." (John 8:31-32 NLT)

So we need to be vigilant to strain out any falsehoods and misinformation we hear and read. Erroneous thinking can clog your mind and spirit and stop the flow of God's influence, power and blessing in your life. And in the same way, we need to set boundaries to prevent harmful things from flowing into our lives: unhealthy relationships, bad habits, compromising situations, unethical business ventures—anything that might stop up the flow of the Holy Spirit in our lives. This should be a no-brainer.

Keep your pipes and your spiritual lifeline free of nasty clogs! "Guard your heart more than anything else, because the source of your life flows from it." (Proverbs 4:23 GWT)

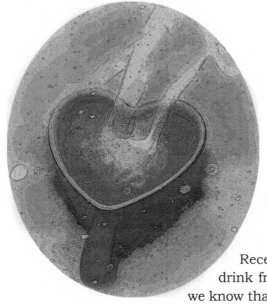

Coffee, Tea, or Me?

Recently, one of us got a drink from the tap. Little did we know that just minutes before, one of us had been doing the dishes—with the hot water running. But now the water in the line was no longer hot. Now it had cooled a bit, so it was only lukewarm. One sip was all it took to realize *it was disgusting!* A cool glass of water is so refreshing, and hot water is truly useful for so many wonderful things—but it was hard to resist spitting out this "in-between" drink!

We started thinking about other beverages that are great either HOT or COLD—but rarely in between. Hot cocoa is delicious when piping hot. And if you refrigerate what's left over, it makes a frosty chocolate drink.

We all know nothing beats a cold glass of lemonade on a scorching summer day; and although we've never tried it, we've heard of people drinking hot lemonade to remedy colds and sore throats.

We suppose there are those who will drink tepid tea or coffee, but most of us can't stand either of these mainstays when they're lukewarm. Coffee or tea that has sat around is gross! On the other hand, both coffee and tea at either end of the "temperature taste" scale are enticing and invigorating. Both are hot libations that comfort us and help us face the day. Iced tea is a mealtime favorite and iced coffee is a guilty pleasure. But in-between, neither of these drinks are very palatable.

There's a silly but cute old made-for-TV movie called *Coffee, Tea or Me?*, which starred Karen Valentine as a daffy airline stewardess looking for a husband. The 1973 movie was loosely based on the novel of the same name, a highly fictionalized account of the "swinging" life of stewardesses, which managed to unfairly stereotype women in this demanding job—and which led to the mainstream adoption of the expression "Coffee, tea or me?"

We mention this because the phrase is perfect for the point we wish to make. Some things, like coffee and tea, are great if they are either HOT or COLD. Otherwise, they're a bit repulsive. In God's eyes—and here's where the "me" part comes in—people are the same way!

Our Heavenly Father delights in us when we're on fire (extremely passionate) for Him. This doesn't mean we go around acting like dorks who can't talk about anything but God. But it does mean our chief focus is on Him and doing His will, and on being pleasing in His sight. It means loving God, and if we love God, then we demonstrate it by doing our utmost to obey Him, and to love others. We'll come up short time and again, but we're constantly trying to rise higher.

If we're cold, God looks down upon us and sees great potential. He loves the non-believer, but He doesn't expect too much from him or her; because God understands that the non-believer doesn't yet know the basics.

The believer doesn't get off quite so easily. God *expects* more because we *know* more and have more. When we accept Christ as our redeemer, we become a member of God's family —and He hopes we'll behave ourselves and not act like a bunch of black sheep.

God can work with people who are *hot* (on fire for God) or *cold* (non-believing with awesome potential), but He doesn't have much use for those of us who are in-between. He actually finds a "lukewarm" believer distasteful: "...Because you are lukewarm—neither hot nor cold—I am about to spit you out of my mouth." (Revelation 3:16 NIV) Scary, right? Like a drink of tepid tea or room-temperature coffee, a half-hearted, unenthusiastic, apathetic, indecisive, wishy-washy believer is *not* very palatable to our Lord.

Are you hot, cold, or lukewarm to God? If your answer is lukewarm, then ask yourself, "What happened to cause me to grow lukewarm?" Have you allowed hurts and disappointments to cool your passion for God? Have you simply grown weary in well-doing? Or have you lost your first love?

You may be attending a local congregation religiously; you may be active in ministry. These things are important, but what God really wants from you is a RELATIONSHIP, not RELIGION. He wants you to love Him, trust in Him, and abide in Him—to do the right thing to please Him, not to fulfill a formula or follow a ritual or be seen by somebody.

If you've allowed your relationship with our Heavenly Father to get tepid, ask Him to relight the fire that was once in you. Return to your first love, and the enthusiasm you once had. Stop sitting on the fence. You can once again be "hot stuff" for the Lord. "Coffee, tea or ME?"

Food for Thought

Not surprisingly, people tend to get passionate about food and cooking. As we wrote in our book *Diet for Dreamers*, Orville Redenbacher had an all-consuming passion for popcorn that lasted his entire life: growing it, popping it, eating it. But most of us are just as guilty as Orville. We enjoy trying new foods and swapping recipes; we may catch ourselves singing the ad jingles for our favorite fast foods; most of us consider dining out at a fine restaurant a major event; and many of us collect cookbooks.

There are television shows and even entire cable channels devoted solely to cooking. (Evidently, watching other people fix stuff to eat is now considered entertainment.) And let's not forget cookbooks. Thin ones and thick ones; general or specialized; written by chefs or homemakers, actors and talk show hosts. Cooks seem to take special pride in displaying their numerous volumes, often on a shelf in the kitchen. And at Christmas or on birthdays, cookbooks frequently show up as gifts. What's this obsession with bound collections of recipes?

Printed cookbooks, previously referred to in Commonwealth English as cookery books, have been around about as

long as printed Bibles. In fact, with the advent of the printing press and movable type, two types of books immediately proliferated: Bibles and cookbooks. Seems odd? Not really. Both deal with food. One for the soul, one for the stomach.

Known collections of recipes date back as far as First-Century Rome. (Can you say *epicurean*?) And by the latter part of the 17th Century, cookery had progressed to an art form, with good cooks in big demand. Many of these "artists" competed with their rivals by publishing their own cookbooks! (The pen *and* the pot are mightier than the sword!)

But it wasn't until the Victorian era—with its preoccupation for domestic respectability—that "cookery writing" began to take the form we recognize today. The first modern cookbook, aimed specifically at the domestic reader, was compiled by Eliza Acton and published in 1845. Her pioneering *Modern Cookery for Private Families* established the format for modern cookbooks, including the now universal practice of listing the ingredients and suggested cooking times with each recipe.

A few more cookbook publication milestones include: *The Boston Cooking School Cookbook*, compiled by the American cook Fannie Farmer (1857–1915) and published in 1896, which contained 1,849 recipes; *The Joy of Cooking* (1931) by Irma Rombauer; and *Mastering the Art of French Cooking* (1961) by Julia Child.

Cookbooks originally contained far more than recipes. They were basic kitchen reference works that included cooking techniques and hosting tips. Think of them as step-by-step survival guides for the domestic cook or homemaker. At the time, however, people usually referred to them as "kitchen bibles"! And that's not an unreasonable comparison. After all, the Word of God and cookbooks, in general, have many similarities. Writers and publishers understand this, which is why we see dozens of books with titles such as *The Cake Bible, The Irish Cooking Bible, The Pizza Bible* and *The Barbecue! Bible.*

The word *bible* is now generally defined as: "handbook, manual, guide, reference, primer, or companion"; because that's exactly what the original, one-and-only Bible is! God's Holy Word is humanity's "bible" for life: a handbook to everyday existence; a guide to love and relationships; a companion for dealing with every problem. It contains all of our Heavenly Father's "recipes" for peace, happiness, security, success and eternal life. In essence, it's the complete account of what God's been cooking up since the creation of the world —and what He's preparing for the future.

Incidentally, the word *bible* comes from the ecclesiastical Latin term *biblia* and translates—literally—as "book." So, when we speak of "The Bible," we're talking about "The Book"—not "*A* book," but rather "*The* Book"!

There are hundreds of new cookbooks published every year. There are *millions* of copies of cookbooks residing in homes. People often refer to them. Many have relied on them to get out of a tight spot in the kitchen. Others frequently give them as gifts. But The Bible trumps ALL these statistics. In fact, The Bible is the #1 bestselling book of all time! So, read it. Get comfortable with it. Learn how to find answers in it. Keep it out on the counter so you can easily refer to it. Give it as a gift. It's God's Holy "Book of Cookery"!

"...It is written, 'THINGS WHICH EYE HAS NOT SEEN AND EAR HAS NOT HEARD, AND WHICH HAVE NOT ENTERED THE HEART OF MAN, ALL THAT GOD HAS PREPARED FOR THOSE WHO LOVE HIM." (1 Corinthians 2:9 NASB)

And just as my Father has granted me a Kingdom, I now grant you the right to eat and drink at my table in my Kingdom.
—Luke 22:29-30 NLT

The Call of the Cookbook!

The similarities between cookbooks and The Bible are fascinating. Books on the "art" of Cookery, as they were once called, were intended as instruction manuals for the kitchen. The Bible is our instruction manual for life, love, and relationships. Cookbooks contain recipes for preparing meals; The Bible contains "recipes" for peace, joy, hope, fulfillment, and eternal life, as well as how to cook up healthy personal relationships.

But the similarities don't stop there! Cookbooks and Bibles have something else in common. There's this great mystique surrounding The Bible. There are people who've never lifted the cover of one, never turned a single page. Many of these people have no idea what "lurks" inside, and may even imagine the contents, if read, might somehow take control of their lives—turning them into mindless puppets. Either they've been listening to the wrong people, or they've been watching way too much science fiction.

To get a reaction from The Bible, just take a copy to class one day, and watch the storm clouds gather over your local school. Place a copy on your desk at work, and you'll witness a wide spectrum of emotions among your coworkers: from smiles to indignation, from people approaching you for advice, to giving you the cold shoulder.

Cookbooks seem to enjoy their own special mystique. Cooks often collect them and take great pride in proudly displaying them. Even people who never cook usually have one or two. They may even leave them out on the kitchen counter —which is sort of like saying, "I don't cook, but I could, if I wanted to." Some homes treat The Bible the same way: they keep this huge ornately bound edition on the coffee table in their living rooms, and someone in the house may even be writing the names and achievements of their family members inside the cover; but they seldom read a word of its printed text.

Of course, who can blame them? Only the Incredible Hulk would be comfortable balancing these monster volumes, let alone reading one in bed. Cookbooks, too, are occasionally printed in "hulked out" editions. We personally own a couple that don't fit on even our largest bookshelves—we have to lay these behemoths flat, and stack other books on top of them! (Warning: if you're actually using one of these "cinderblocks" while cooking, be sure your hands are free of any oil or butter residues; if you accidentally drop one of these cookbooks on your toes, it won't be the onions making you cry!)

And everybody seems to want to write a cookbook. It doesn't matter if you're already a famous talk show host, an award-winning performer, an accomplished athlete, or even British Royalty. Apparently, you haven't really arrived until you've written a cookbook. The countless celebrities who've published cookbooks include: singers Olivia Newton-John, Frank Sinatra, and Isaac Hayes ("Can you dig it?"); George Foreman; the Chicago Cubs; poet Maya Angelou; actors Gwyneth Paltrow, Stanley Tucci, Sophia Loren, Paul Newman, and Morgan Freeman ("Didn't you get the memo?"); comedian Jeff Foxworthy; weatherman Al Roker; talk show hosts Regis and Kathie Lee; Jerry Seinfeld's wife, Jessica (We're not sure, but her book might be about nothing); Sarah Ferguson, the Duchess of York; and even Miss Piggy. (Sorry, no pork recipes.)

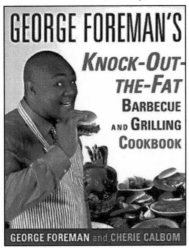

But you don't need to be a celebrity to publish a cookbook. Thousands of self-published cookbooks are distributed yearly, by civic groups, faith congregations, historical societies, law enforcement agencies, fire departments, schools, and even individual families. Chef's put out cookbooks. National fast food chains and many regional restaurants have their names on cookbooks. Well-known brands such as Betty Crocker and Hershey's publish cookbooks. There are even cookbooks tied to specific products such as Kraft Cream Cheese and Heinz Ketchup. (Seriously?) TV shows even have cookbooks! *The Sopranos*, *Gilligan's Island*, and *The Andy Griffith Show*, to name a few.

Soooo many people have written *soooo* many cookbooks. Not even Carl Sagan could've comprehended the numbers: "Billions and billions...." These "kitchen bibles" are collected and proudly displayed; given as gifts and sold at garage sales. Ironically, only a small percentage of these books are actually read. Even fewer are actually used. So, of what benefit are they? You can't learn to cook by telepathy. Unless you open the book and read it, unless you use the recipes inside, it becomes nothing more than a knick-knack. And the same can be said of The Bible.

Many of us proudly display the Bible in our homes. We carry a copy under our arms to Church and prayer meetings. We're comforted to see it on the nightstand in our hotel rooms, or in the waiting rooms of our doctors' offices. But how many of us actually refer to its many wonderful "recipes" for peace, happiness, and security? How many of us use it as our moral compass? Remember, no "cookbook"—whether about food for the stomach or food for the spirit—can help you unless ... *you use it!*

> *Study this Book of Instruction continually. Meditate on it day and night so you will be sure to obey everything written in it. Only then will you prosper and succeed in all you do.*
> —Joshua 1:8 NLT

Many Motives for Countless Cookbooks!

Like many people, we're passionate about food. Yeah, that's a euphemistic way of saying, "We love to eat!" But our passion isn't just prompted by our stomachs. We're two information junkies. We're also certified (*certifiable?*) bibliophiles, with a house filled with hundreds of books on countless subjects. Among our many books is an extensive and fascinating collection of publications surveying the history of food, dining, table customs, and related topics. And copious cookbooks—including a few just too weird not to be wonderful, such as *Cooking Out of this World*, which collects recipes by famous science fiction writers. But our library of cookbooks is rather small compared to the collections of other, more fanatical aficionados.

People buy and collect cookbooks for a variety of reasons. (1) Some people actually want the recipes. We can appreciate this. Cookbooks offer a window to other cultures, and a door to trying other cuisines. These collectors, like us, probably love to cook and try new things. We previously mentioned the similarities between cookbooks and the Word of God, and the same reasoning applies to The Bible. The Holy Scriptures are filled with "recipes" for hope, peace, joy and security—basically everything we need for abundant life. The Bible also affords a window on another, spiritual, lifestyle. It's essentially our door to eternal life.

(2) Some people buy cookbooks that tie into a special interest they share. There are historical cookbooks for history

buffs, such as *Lobscouse and Spotted Dog* (recipes for foods served in Nelson's Navy, circa 1812); cookbooks that transport readers to other lands such as Thailand or the Mediterranean; cookbooks that connect to interesting subcultures or ethnic groups, such as *Taste of Tremé: Creole, Cajun, and Soul Food from New Orleans' Famous Neighborhood.*

Similarly, historians have read the Word of God to learn about Biblical times. And if anyone is interested in God's spiritual subculture or the "ethnic" group we call the People of Faith, then look no further than the Bible.

(3) Sometimes readers are simply interested in the person who "wrote" the cookbook, assuming that person actually did. We discussed celebrities who've penned cookbooks. Oprah and Dr. Phil are two more we can add to an interminable list of "authors"! Finding out their favorite foods helps us to better know the celebrities whose lives we follow. God wrote the Bible. True, He used a "ghostwriter"—the *Holy* Ghost, also called the Holy Spirit, who works through people and "guides us into all truths." (John 14:17)

Want a "celebrity cookbook"? God is greater than the most talented actor starring in the biggest budget Hollywood action movie: not only does God perform all His own stunts, *His* "special effects" are real and not computer generated!

(4) People also buy cookbooks because they've seen the author on television. Here, the idea is that if we like Emeril's or Rachael Ray's cooking shows, we'll also like their books. If you get inspired watching *The 700 Club* or TBN's *Praise the Lord* or DayStar's *Table Talk*, you'll want to grab the "tie-in" book: *The Bible.*

(5) Cookbooks make nice gifts for any occasion, especially when you're not sure what else to give the person. Everyone needs the Word of God, so The Bible is the ultimate no-brainer gift!

(6) Some people are simply into collecting, and cookbooks seem to be popular—even for those who don't cook. These collectors proudly display their cookbooks on the shelf, sometimes for status—like trophies gathering dust. People often treat the Bible the same way. It languishes on a coffee table, unread, and hence does the "collector" no good. Every house,

hotel room, and waiting room should have a Bible, but it should never be reduced to the status of a "decoration"; it's not designed to impress visitors with one's "spirituality"—it's designed to help us live Spirit-filled lives.

Some people are "fans" of Jesus Christ, and they've bought His "cookbook." But they're not necessarily followers of Jesus: people who *read* His Word, are *transformed* by it, and then seek to do the Father's will. Religious people *carry* their Bibles to church. People of Faith *read* it daily.

The Bible is translated into every known language and read by every people group. It's available on CD and DVD, and has been the source material for many movies and TV shows. It's God's love letter to His people—ALL the people of earth, regardless of ethnicity or nationality. One BOOK for one RACE—the *human* race. As Jesus Christ stated, "It is written: *Man shall not live on bread alone, but on every word that comes from the mouth of God.*'" (Matthew 4:4 NIV; Read also Deuteronomy 8:3)

How sweet your words taste to me; they are sweeter than honey. Your commandments give me understanding....
Your word is ... a light for my path.
—Psalm 119:103-105 NLT

Let the word of Christ dwell in you richly,
teaching and admonishing...in all wisdom....
—Colossians 3:16 ESV

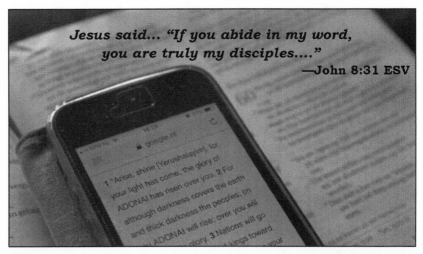

Jesus said... "If you abide in my word, you are truly my disciples...."
—John 8:31 ESV

Wanna See Something Really Weird?

We've discussed in the last three chapters, the mystique of cookbooks, and compared certain aspects of the cookbook to the Bible. Before we shelve this topic, we want to cover the subject of unusual if not downright WEIRD cookbooks.

We previously mentioned that a group of science fiction authors—not the usual type of people who write cookbooks—collaborated on a collection of recipes and called it *Cooking Out of this World*. And like the plots in many of their novels, some of these recipes were pretty far-fetched. "Old Prospector's Coffee" was totally outrageous, and the creator of that one humorously warned readers *not* to drink this nasty brew. But as far as bizarre cookbooks are concerned, this compilation of SF-related recipes was fairly run-of-the-mill.

Sometimes the thing that makes a cookbook truly weird, is its author. The legendary stage and film actor Vincent Price, who was unfairly typecast as the evil, often monstrous, villain

in a long string of horror movies, loved to cook and collect recipes from the many places he visited. Seeing the name of the man who scared us silly in such classics as *The House on Haunted Hill* and *The Tingler*, on the cover of a "book of cookery" seems a little bizarre—at first glance; but Price was a gentle and refined soul who loved good food, and was nothing like the sinister characters he portrayed.

We're not sure we can say the same of John Poister's *The Pyromaniac's Cookbook*. The author suggests that everything tastes better after you set it on fire. Seriously? Apart from recipes compiled by questionable cooks, there are also those that call for some rather nasty ingredients. We're not fans of creepy-crawlies, so *The Eat a Bug Cookbook: Real Recipes Using Beetles, Spiders, and Other Truly Unusual Ingredients*, by David George Gordon, sends shivers up our spines—as well as feelings of nausea.

Not quite as bad, but just as unappetizing, is Buck Peterson's *The Original Roadkill Cookbook*, which features recipes for such "delicacies" as Pavement Possum! Since we have no desire to ever try these dishes, we'll never know if they taste BAD; but we do know they are in BAD taste!

There are also several legitimate cookbooks out there that just *sound* bad. *Cooking with Poo* is one. It's written by Saiyuud Diwong, and has nothing to do with what first comes to most minds—Khun Poo runs a famous Thai cooking school. And there are also cookbooks that call for unconventional cooking methods, such as *Manifold Destiny*, written by Chris Maynard and featuring recipes you cook on a hot automobile engine block!

There are plenty of other crazy cookbooks out there. Some are in such poor taste as to not be worth mentioning. And yeah, we *know* that many of these are simply designed to be funny. But when there's a really bad cookbook, written by someone who's not a good cook and often not at all serious about food or its preparation, it can—pardon the pun—leave a bad taste in the reader's mouth.

Even with legitimate cookbooks, if the recipes are too time-consuming or difficult to prepare, if they call for ingredients that are too exotic or too expensive, and if the resultant dish isn't very palatable, it can be a real turnoff to people who genuinely want to learn more about the kitchen, cooking and different foods. Word of advice to would-be cookbook writers who know nothing about *good* cooking: leave the subject alone. Please find another way to make your friends nauseous. We don't need any more spurious recipes.

The same can be said of the Bible. If you're writing or speaking about God's doctrines, be sure you yourself fully understand the truth of His Word. Be careful not to turn people off to the Good News of salvation through Jesus Christ. Be a "sound copy" of God's message, a "living epistle," as the Apostle Paul called it. Face it, we're the only "Bibles" some people will ever "read!"

And if you're searching for information about God, read the ONLY "authorized" book on the subject—The Bible. Don't take people's opinions as gospel. Don't take single passages of the Scriptures out of context. Don't overemphasize a single verse, or try to use it to justify a bizarre doctrine or peculiar practice. Don't listen to the half-truths of cults composed of misguided people. Don't ignore a clear verse in order to be politically correct, or to justify some personal philosophy or lifestyle you have.

And *please*, don't consult works of fiction when looking for truths about our Lord and the Word of God. Novels such as *The Da Vinci Code* are highly *inaccurate* at best; but at worst, these books are purposely deceptive and misleading— they *are*, after all, just works of *fiction!* Oh, and one last thing, it's hard to learn how to cook just by consulting a cookbook. The best cooks learned from other good cooks. So find someone who's learned to "rightly divide [accurately explain and correctly handle] the Word of God" (2 Timothy 2:15)—and learn from them. Pastors, priests, rabbis, chaplins, missionaries or Sunday school teachers are all a great place to start. These people "hold classes" in churches and synagogues, and use the Bible as their textbook. *These people can cook!*

Now the Holy Spirit tells us clearly that ... some will turn away from the true faith; they will follow deceptive spirits and teachings that come from demons.
—1 Timothy 4:1 NLT

Do not be carried away by all kinds of strange teachings.
—Hebrews 13:9 NIV

Be on guard so that you will not be carried away by the errors of these wicked people and lose your own secure footing.
—2 Peter 3:17 NLT

The Beauty of Baking!

We've defined the "Junk Food" of life, those guilty pleasures in which we frequently overindulge—such as TV, sports, video games, etc.—and how we need to balance our "diet" with healthier fare: specifically, reading the Word of God. We've also discussed spiritual "processed food"—Christian music, Sunday school lessons, inspirational TV shows, etc.—we often consume too much of, instead of turning to a more pure, unadulterated source of spiritual nutrition: specifically (ahem) reading the Word of God. We'll now explain something that goes hand in hand with these topics: the beauty of baking!

Baking isn't as easy as preparing other types of foods, for a few simple reasons. First, you usually have to stick to the instructions! And follow them in order! Plus, you shouldn't add anything that's not listed. Or subtract anything. Or substitute anything. It's like a science. Deviate from the proven formula and the cake may fall, the pie may turn out pathetic.

Despite the number of cookbooks sold each year, most cooks rarely refer to written instructions of any kind. They just walk into the kitchen and do their own thing. They stand in front of the range and start to boogie, waving a big spoon in one hand, while shaking out spices with other.

When cooking veggies, for instance, it's easy to toss in some extra butter and seasonings. And as a result, the dish is usually greatly improved. Cooks tend to do a lot of this sort of thing. They stir the broth, taste it, and then decide it needs something. They add a teaspoon of this and a sprinkle of that.

If they're whipping up one of their favorite recipes and they don't have one of the necessary ingredients, they improvise! Through experience, they've learned that they can make smart substitutions and sometimes even leave stuff out. Or add stuff—strictly in the name of science—like an extra stick of butter! Generally, the dish turns out just as tasty, perhaps even better. But if you try to do this when baking, you're courting disaster.

Life is NOT like cooking. We often approach it, however, as though it were. In our relationships, our ways of thinking and behaving, we act like we can do our own thing and everything will magically turn out okay. We improvise, make substitutions, leave stuff out, and throw stuff in. We often don't refer to God's recipe for success in life.

Life is like baking. If we want it to turn out right, we need to follow the directions—in order. So where do "bakers" turn for instruction? Specifically ... the Word of God. (Betcha didn't see *that* one coming.) Moreover, when following God's instructions, you can't leave anything out, or add anything, or make substitutions. So. Just. Follow. The directions!

No baker worth his or her flour ever deviates from what works, and then wonders why their bread is dry or chewy or looks like a gooey mess on the inside. They follow instructions and have great success. (Baker's Joy?) And that, dear friends, is the simplicity and the sheer Beauty of Baking!

Moral of this little analogy? When in the kitchen, have fun, sling the spices, do your own thing. But in life, follow the instructions in the Holy Scriptures. That way you'll experience the Baker's Joy!

Be careful to obey all the instructions Moses gave you.
Do not deviate from them, turning either to the right or to
the left. Then you will be successful in everything you do.
—Joshua 1:7 NLT

Just Follow the Recipe!

As we stated, there are many similarities between cookbooks and the Bible. For instance, cookbooks are collections of recipes created to help us prepare successful meals; the Bible is a book of recipes created to help us prepare for a successful life. The recipes in most cookbooks were tested in the kitchen of the author. God is the author of the Bible, and He's tested all His "recipes" in the kitchen of life! Interestingly, the standard format for culinary recipes is not much different from the format of the successful life recipes God gives us in His holy Word.

The standard format for a cookbook recipe really should be a no-brainer, but it wasn't until the Victorian era that a writer struck upon the idea. Between 1857 and 1861, Mrs. Isabella Beeton wrote 24 installments of a guide to maintaining a proper home. She later collected and published these as *Mrs. Beeton's Book of Household Management*, a monstrous volume of over 1100 pages. Her *hulking* hardcover contained 900 recipes, so readers often referred to it as "Mrs. Beeton's Cookbook." It was the first cookbook to establish a logical format for recipes, a format which is still used today.

In order for the reader to easily follow them, and not leave out any steps or ingredients, recipes should be formatted as follows: (1) a list of all ingredients needed—and their specific measurements or quantities—and (2) the precise steps to follow while preparing the recipe—in the exact order the steps must be performed!

Try to prepare a dessert that leaves out an important ingredient, such as "a tablespoon of vanilla extract," and unless you're a mind reader, you'll end up with something very different from what you set out to make. And if you frequently use cookbooks, you probably already know how frustrating it is to be following the directions of a recipe, and realize a step is missing or out of order. If we're supposed to add melted butter to beaten egg whites, please don't wait to tell us to beat the eggs AFTER we've already melted the butter—or we might decide to just beat you instead.

The God of the Universe knows that "all things should be done decently and in order." (1 Corinthians 14:40) In His Word, He lists all the ingredients you need to have success in every area of life. And He lists the steps we must follow in the proper order. God's recipes for peace, contentment, security and success are properly "formatted"! Below is an example.

God's recipe for *Keeping Our Priorities Straight* (with all the ingredients and steps listed in order):

1. *You must love the LORD your God*
    a. *with all your heart,*
    b. *all your soul,*
    c. *and all your mind.*

This is the first and greatest commandment. A second is equally important:

2. Love your neighbor as yourself. The entire law and all the demands of the prophets are based on these two commandments. (Matthew 22:37-39 NLT)

[This "recipe" follows the same order as the Ten Commandments: the initial commandments deal with our relationship with God the Father; the remaining commandments deal with our relationships with those around us. Read it and you'll see!]

3. ...First, be concerned about:
   a. His kingdom and
   b. what has His approval.
   c. Then all these things will be provided for you.
                                    (Matthew 6:33 GWT)

4.   a. Trust in the LORD and do good;
      b. Dwell in the land and cultivate faithfulness.

5.   a. Delight yourself in the LORD;
      b. And He will give you the desires of your heart.
                                    (Psalm 37:4 NASB)

6. So place yourselves under God's authority.

7.   a. Resist the devil,
      b. and he will run away from you.

8.   a. Come close to God,
      b. and he will come close to you. (James 4:7-8 GWT)

Follow this recipe and then God and His desires will be the focus of your life. You'll keep your priorities in order—something which will be reflected in how you start your day and spend your time, as well as your talents and resources. Follow this recipe and you'll be cooking up some good success in all you do.

The Secret Ingredient

To quote the Pillsbury Doughboy, "Nothin' says lovin' like something from the oven"! That's the idea behind the recipe for Amish Friendship Bread, a sweet, stirred quick-bread with a cake-like texture and a mild cinnamon flavor. The reason it's called friendship bread is because the recipe calls for a cup of sourdough starter (a mixture of yeast, flour, sugar and milk) which is shared among friends in much the same way as a chain letter—only with tastier results. Here's how it works:

Someone first adds a package of dry yeast (dissolved in a little warm water) to one cup each of flour, sugar, and milk. The yeast mixture begins to ferment, but for the yeast to remain active, the mixture must be "fed" every 5 days by adding another cup each of flour, sugar, and milk. On the tenth day, the starter is ready for use, but there's FIVE cups of the stuff! Solution: use one cup of starter to bake a loaf of delicious bread, give away three cups of starter to friends (who then begin their own 10-day cycle), and save the last cup of starter to begin the next cycle.

So every tenth day, a person either has to bake 4 loaves of friendship bread or connect with 3 new friends who don't already have starter. Obviously, the process can continue forever, and eventually the starter spreads through entire communities. A sweet idea!

No one's absolutely sure who started this tradition. Elizabeth Coblentz, a member of the Old Order Amish and the author of *The Amish Cook*, writes that true Amish friendship bread is "just sourdough bread that is passed around to the sick and needy." That's still pretty sweet. When we shared God's recipe for Keeping Your Priorities Straight, it boiled down to:

(1) *Love the LORD... with all your heart, soul, and mind (which is the first and greatest commandment) and then* (2) *love your neighbor as yourself.* (Matthew 22:37-38) Clearly the secret ingredient in God's favorite recipe is LOVE. And as we previously stated, love makes everything in life taste better.

Love is the "starter" for God's special brand of "friendship bread." He commands us to share it until it's spread throughout our world. In the verse above—specifically, the second half of "Keeping our Priorities Straight"—God commands us to love others to the same degree we love ourselves. That's some seriously intense affection, folks. It reminds us of what we traditionally refer to as "The Golden Rule," which is a distillation of Matthew 7:12 (GWT): "Always do for other people everything you want them to do for you. That is [the meaning of] Moses' Teachings and the Prophets."

In other words, if you want people to be kind to you, show you respect, and be sensitive to your needs, then you must also do these same things for others—be they black, white, red, or polka-dotted; male, female, young, old, rich, poor, or what have you. We are never closer to God or more like Him than when we love others: "God is love, and all who live in love live in God, and God lives in them." (1 John 4:16 NLT)

It's not always easy. We can all be a little unlovable at times. So we need to try to understand what other people are going through. We need to try to see things from their perspective. And when we honestly disagree with someone, we need to do so lovingly and without disrespecting the person. "Speak the truth in love...." (Ephesians 4:15 NLT) Your homework for today is to read 1 Corinthians 13, the "love chapter"; then go out and share some starter—LOVE!

That Tears It!

In "Leeked Out" we discussed some things onions have in common with life experiences and human relationships. For instance, each day we peel back another layer of the "onion" to reveal new mysteries, new opportunities, new lessons. And in our relationships, we again need to peel back the layers that insulate people from each other.

Interestingly, living and interacting with people is exactly like cutting into an onion! The experience will often make you cry! We all know how the pain and disappointments of life and relationships can leave us in tears, but why exactly do onions make us cry? Simple answer: it's Chemistry!

When you slice an onion, you break the plant cells, releasing amino acid sulfoxides. No need to remember this, it won't be on the test. These newly released amino acids form sulfenic acids, which in turn mix with enzymes in the onion to produce a volatile sulfur compound. As this sulfur compound pervades the kitchen air, it quickly gets into the eyes, where it reacts with the natural moisture to produce a mild solution of ... SULFURIC ACID!!! *Gaahh!!* No wonder it stings! This is the type of acid found in car batteries (albeit, far less concentrated). Our tears are quickly released to flush out the irritant.

111

They are a natural, God-given mechanism for relieving the burning sensation of onion vapor.

Similarly, our emotional tears help to relieve some of the pain of life's disappointments. And just as the presence of an irritant signals the eyes to tear, our emotional tears alert God that we need an extra dollop of His grace and comfort.

You see, we have a personal, loving God who deeply cares for us, and He pays close attention when we suffer. No pain, hurt or disappointment goes unnoticed. God takes a full accounting of your emotional stress, that He may comfort you in those moments: "You keep track of all my sorrows. You have collected all my tears in your bottle. You have recorded each one in your book?" (Psalm 56:8 NLT)

If you're hurting today, seek the Lord in prayer. Cry out to the one whom Isaiah 53:3-4 describes as "despised and rejected—a man of sorrows, acquainted with deepest grief. ...It was our weaknesses He carried; it was our sorrows that weighed Him down." (NIV)

We all have sorrows. We each face trials that bring us pain. We learn from these hard times, and through them we grow closer to God. But God has also promised to bring an end to our suffering. "...He will wipe away every tear from their eyes, and death shall be no more, neither shall there be mourning, nor crying, nor pain anymore...." (Rev 21:4 ESV)

God made us several promises. Claim them! "...You will weep no more. How gracious the LORD will be to you at the sound of your cry! As soon as he hears it, he will answer you." (Isaiah 30:19 ISV) "Weeping may endure for a night, but Joy comes in the morning." (Psalm 30:5 NKJV)

"Those who sow in tears will reap in joy." (Psalm 126:5 NKJV) Life got you down? Hurting in a relationship? Chopping onions? Cry out to the Lord, "The Father of mercies, and the God of all comfort." (2 Corinthians 1:3 NKJV)

A Hair-Raising Tale?

Forget about Frankenstein's monster or the Creature from the Black Lagoon! These guys are actually kind of sympathetic characters. *Hey*, wanna see something *really* scary?

It's a cook's worst nightmare, something no one ever wants to see in real life! Is it that multi-legged cockroach that invaded your kitchen after stowing away in the bag of potatoes you just brought home? *Shudder!* Is it the trail of ants leading from the window, to that apple pie cooling on the counter, now covered with a seething swarm of hungry insects! *Shiver!* No, it's something far more terrifying, something far more insidious. It's ... *gasp!* ... a human hair! Found where it's not supposed to be: curled up on someone's plate, lurking in a serving dish; peeking out from a casserole! *Gahh-rosss!!*

A stray hair in the kitchen or at the dining room table is not a pretty sight. Which is why chefs take precautions to keep their hair from getting into the food by wearing those cool, poufy white hats. Cafeteria cooks are often seen wearing hair nets. And in our home, Wilma, who's got tons of thick long black hair, carefully gathers it back in a ponytail that would make Mister Ed swoon, and ties it off before entering the kitchen—lest she violate a universal law of cooking! Let's face it, seeing a hair in the food can kill your appetite! *Oh, the horror!*

Ed: Wilbur, I found a hair in my feedbag. Made me sick!
Wilbur: Okay, Ed. I'll wear a hairnet.

MGM Television

Hair. And *horror.* Two things that got us thinking. Not long ago, Wilma was

If you're going to cook those, will you *please* wear a hairnet! (Universal Studios)

encouraging a friend who had some frightful ideas about God. To set the record straight, she had to point out a few facts about our Heavenly Father. First off, God is not a holy terror just waiting for us to make a mistake so He can rain down fire upon us like the dragon Smaug in *The Hobbit.* Nor is He this strange, distant, impersonal alien entity, who just for kicks decided to create the universe, earth and people, and then abandoned His creation, leaving us to fend for ourselves.

Quite the contrary, the loving God of the Bible, the God of Abraham, Isaac and Israel, who took on human form (in order to better relate to us) and walked the earth as Jesus Christ, cares about each of us deeply. We previously discussed how God is vigilant to our sufferings. He's moved by our sorrows, "He collects our tears in a bottle" that He may comfort us in times of trouble. (Psalm 56:8 NLT)

Furthermore, our Heavenly Father is not a dead-beat dad. He didn't create us and then walk out the door. "God is not human, that he should lie; not a human being, that he should change his mind. Does he speak and then not act?" (Numbers 23:19 NIV) *Never!*

Indeed, "...God has said, 'Never will I leave you; never will I forsake you.'" (Hebrews 13:5) And the Psalmist wrote, "Even if my father and mother abandon me, the Lord will hold me close." (Psalm 27:10 NLT)

How close does God hold us? Close enough to gather every tear. How much does God care about you? Enough that He wants to be with you *all the time,* involved in every aspect of your life. God is so observant, so personal, so caring, so concerned, and values you so much, that He even numbers "the hairs on your head"! (Matthew 10:30)

Which brings us back to the beginning of this chapter: speaking figuratively, with God being this careful about you, you'll never have to fear a "stray hair" in life. God is watching over you and HE CARES! Cling to His promises. Run to His loving arms! "Give all your worries and cares to God, for He cares about you." (1 Peter 5:7 NKJV)

God and Groceries!

We always keep a shopping list in the kitchen. It's a long note-pad with a nifty little magnet on the back, which allows us to post it on Fridgey's door. You remember Fridgey, don't you? He's our refrigerator. No, we're not loony, just sentimental; and we're telling you about our shopping list to illustrate an important characteristic of our Lord.

We keep our list handy, posted where we can easily see it, and we frequently update it. Whenever we're cooking and notice we're getting low on sugar or milk or what have you, we immediately add it to our ever growing list. We learned a long time ago that if we don't write it down while we're think-ing about it, we may forget it altogether. When we shop for groceries we want to make it count. We don't want to come home without everything we needed.

So before we go to the market, we grab our list containing all the stuff we jotted down during the week. Because nothing is more aggravating than coming home, putting away the groceries, and then starting dinner, only to realize we forgot the oregano for the spaghetti sauce! When something like that happens, because sometimes we do forget to write down an item on our list, we either have to make an extra trip to the market, wasting time and gas, or change our menu plans.

We've gotten pretty good at updating our list, though. So we don't usually forget what we need. But we gotta have our list! And guess what? God keeps a list, too! What's God need a list for? So He will remember what He needs. What could God possibly need? He needs us! He created us to have fellowship with Him, and that's exactly what He wants. In a manner of speaking, we're on God's shopping list. In Luke 10:20, the "Great Physician" proclaims to anyone who puts his or her faith in Christ, "Rejoice, because your names are written in heaven." (KJB)

God has His own list, and He will never forget us. God keeps close track of His list, jotting down our names, constantly remembering us: "...I have written your name on the palms of my hands." (Isaiah 49:16 NLT) Think about it for a moment: when someone really wants to remember something, like an important phone number, they often write it on their hand. It's safer than a piece of paper, which can get misplaced. But when something's written on your hand, you're definitely going to see it ... repeatedly!

Bottom line: God has *not* forgotten you and He never will! He's got a list. Ask Him to put your name on it.

"...This is what the Lord says, the One who created you... 'Do not be afraid, because I've redeemed you. I've called you by name; you are Mine.'" (Isaiah 43:1 ISV)

Knowing that foods and other items in the kitchen have expiration dates and can go bad, the authors contemplate their annual spring cleaning.

No Expiration Date

Each spring, dozens of hummingbirds arrive at our home. These tiny creatures hang out with us every year, from April to around mid-September, to sip nectar from the six feeders we hang outside our windows.

Their arrival reminds us it's time for Spring Cleaning, an opportunity to clean up, fix up, and freshen up! Yes, when spring arrives everything starts looking up! We take the opportunity to also reorganize our kitchen shelves, exchanging our festive winter place-settings, which feature wild birds, for brighter plates depicting songbirds. (Yes, we LOVE birds!)

We also go through the pantry to check the expiration dates on canned and boxed goods. We try to use up food items that are close to expiring, and toss anything that's gone out of date. We hope you, too, frequently check the expiration dates on foods in your kitchen, because one of life's sad truths is that everything we buy to prepare our families' meals has a pre-determined shelf life. (You're gonna love where we're heading with this analogy, but first....)

Just a couple weeks ago, we heard a news story about a sweet 77-year-old Italian lady who inadvertently poisoned her son and three grandchildren, ages 8 to 12, all because she was oblivious to the expiration date on some packets of hot cocoa. Her "victims" fell ill to vomiting and diarrhea, and soon ended up in the emergency room where they were treated for food poisoning! Turns out the cocoa had expired ... 25 years ago! But what's amazing is that we don't hear about this sort of thing more often.

Life is hectic, so who has time to pay attention to all those tiny dates printed in often obscure places on the labels of the foods we buy? And because it's generally out of sight, all the stuff hiding in the farthest reaches of our kitchen cabinets, is also generally out of mind. Who knows what evil lurks in the shadows of the cupboard shelves! Flour and breadcrumbs can harbor grub worms, jars can lose their vacuum and grow mold. And in the refrigerator...oh, the horrors of out-of-date dairy products! Even the nectar we put out for our hummers has to be changed daily when it's hot (and the feeders cleaned), or bacteria harmful to the birds will start to grow.

So, unless we want to poison the people we love, we need to check the dates! Unless we want the promise of a comforting mug of hot chocolate to turn into a trip to the doctor, we need to take stock of our shelves at least once a year and the fridge about weekly.

How often should we take stock of God's promises? Daily is wonderful, because we can all use a daily helping of encouragement. But unlike food, God's promises don't come with expiration dates. Our Heavenly Father is into long-term agreements. In fact, His covenants and commitments are "everlasting"! He keeps His promises. Period! "O LORD, God of Israel, there is no God like you in all of heaven and earth. You keep your covenant and show unfailing love to all who walk before you in wholehearted devotion." (2 Chronicles 6:14 NLT)

"Your kingdom is an everlasting kingdom, and your dominion endures through all generations. The LORD is trustworthy in all he promises and faithful in all he does." (Psalm 145:13 NIV)

God's love doesn't have a limited shelf life. *His Love, Mercy, and Grace stay FRESH!*

"Great is His faithfulness; his mercies begin afresh each morning." (Lamentations 3:23 NLT) "I have loved you, my people, with an everlasting love. With unfailing love I have drawn you to myself." (Jeremiah 31:3 NLT)

Claim God's fresh, eternally-lasting promises today! They never get stale or go bad!

Crock Pot Promises

In this age of high-speed internet, fast food, express checkout, and technology bent on making people and processes move ever more quickly, it's really cool to learn about something that was actually designed to be slow. We're talking about the crock pot; designed to allow cooks to safely prepare a soup, stew or roast at a lower heat, while they were doing something else—probably away from home. In fact, one clever ad slogan announced that the Crock Pot "cooks all day while the cook's away"!

At this point, we should explain that *all* Crock Pots are slow cookers, but not all slow cookers are crock pots. *Huh?* You see, Crock-Pot is a brand name, in the same way that Jell-O is a brand of jello—*ahem*, gelatin!

Rival's Crock Pot was *the* first commercially marketed slow cooker. Initially it was marketed toward working moms who could toss meat and veggies in the pot before heading out the door, and then return home hours later to a hot cooked meal. The Crock Pot sold millions throughout the 1970s, but then it seems to have fallen out of fashion. Perhaps it's image as a slow cooker no longer fit in with the hyper-driven lifestyles of a newer, speed-obsessed generation.

Well, baby, the crock pot is back! And we're not ashamed to tell you we own seven of them! We use them for a variety of food preparations, and particularly during our Annual Soup

Social. We plan it for winter, then invite friends and family to join us for a meal featuring three or four hearty soups and stews. Our guests often pitch in by bringing their favorite breads or specialty crackers. The neat thing about having several crock pots lining the kitchen counter is that our guests can help themselves to as much soup as they want, as often as they want; and the soup stays hot!

Irving Naxon invented the first slow cooker way back in 1936, and called it the Naxon Beanery. In 1970, he sold the Beanery to the Rival Company, which quickly changed the name to the Crock Pot. (Can't imagine why.) But where'd Irving ever get the idea for the slow-cooker in the first place? The answer may come as a pleasantly surprise.

Many Sunday-go-to-meeting families owe the delicious hot dinner that awaited them after church services, to Irving's Jewish mother, the Sabbath, and ... *beans!*

Irving's mom often told him about a bean stew called *cholent*, which she made back home in Lithuania. She explained to her son that on the Jewish Sabbath, the day of rest, observant Jews aren't supposed to do any work—including cooking. But cholent slow-cooked all by itself. The stew went on the fire a little before sun-down on Friday night. At sun-down, the time the Sabbath begins, the ovens were turned off. Pots of cholent were placed inside the ovens, and the residual heat, over the course of 24 hours—all the way until the end of Saturday's Shabbat services the next day—would be enough to complete the cooking process.

Sometimes the answers to our prayers are like cholent; the results are wonderful but not immediate. The process of realizing our goals, or seeing our hopes and dreams come to fruition, is *slow*. It takes time to find and marry your soul mate. The birth of a child comes after 9 months of expecting. It can take years to develop a good career, decades to fulfill a dream. But we need to develop "Crock Pot Patience"! We need to learn to toss our cares and prayers into God's hands and then get on with the rest our lives, confident that the answers, the breakthroughs, the blessings are being prepared—slow-cooked to perfection, while we're taking care of other things God wants us to do.

In the Bible, David and Joseph waited years to see their dreams fulfilled. Moses, Joshua, and Caleb all waited decades to achieve their goals. Abraham and Sarah didn't receive their Isaac, "the son of Promise," until after a quarter-century had passed. But all these heroes of God's Word had something in common. Call it "cholent confidence": the process may be long, but it works ... and the results are pleasing indeed! "...The LORD says: At just the right time, I will respond to you." (Isaiah 49:8 NLT)

The Lord isn't really being slow about his promise, as some people think. No, he is being patient for your sake.
—2 Peter 3:9 NLT

Write the vision; make it plain.... For still the vision awaits its appointed time; ...If it seems slow, wait for it; it will surely come.... —Habakkuk 2:2-3 ESV

An Air-Tight Promise!

There are many brands of resealable plastic storage containers sold in stores today. Most are designed to go from refrigerator to microwave and then, if necessary, back to the refrigerator. These containers come in all shapes and sizes, and some of them have very specific functions. Some are made of a durable plastic that can withstand repeated use in the microwave as well as countless trips through the dishwasher. Some are pricey, but there are a few brands that are made of a thinner plastic and intended to be semi-disposable, such as Gladware.

These cheaper containers can be reused several times before repeated microwaving leaves them whimpering for mercy and—like a few friends we know—all bent out shape. Few people refer to these food-savers as "resealable plastic storage containers"; it's a lot easier to refer to them collectively as *tupperware.*

Tupperware, however, is a brand name. But since Tupperware were the first and most popular food storage containers, many people use the famous name to describe any similar product—in the same way most people call all gelatin Jello, and all tissues Kleenex. Perhaps wrong, but understandable. Tupperware paved the way and made work in the kitchen easier. These marvels of versatility also empowered women who were stuck in the kitchen. More on this later.

A Massachusetts chemist named Earl Silas Tupper (1907–83) had invented a soft but rugged plastic in 1938, but he wasn't too sure what would be its best use until he came up with the idea for Tupperware in 1946. Tupper initially developed his soon-to-be famous containers to store food and keep it fresh. His first design was a bell-shaped container called the *Wonderlier Bowl.* Not only did the Wonderlier keep food fresh, but it also could be used as a serving bowl.

Tupperware was also a pioneer of direct marketing. During WWII, thousands of women entered the workplace, filling jobs in factories and offices. By the 1950s most of them had returned to the kitchen, and many of them were feeling a bit shut in, underused, and forgotten. The Tupperware Party allowed these women an opportunity to once again be a part of the business world, to interact and to earn money. And all for a product they could get passionate about.

What made Tupperware so special? When the containers were sealed, they were airtight, so foods stayed fresher—for a much longer period. Tupperware boasted its containers were so airtight, that once you sealed one, you could crack open a small section of the lid and "burp" out the remaining air. Tupperware even went so far as to patent their "burping seal"! In their ads, Tupperware boasted the "airtight promise"!

Freshness and flavors were locked in, and liquids couldn't seep out around the lid.

Why are we gushing so much over a plastic container? We're not. When first introduced, Tupperware's Airtight Promise was indeed innovative. Tupperware sealed tight as a drum. It locked in freshness. It preserved what was inside. But if you're like us, and you've trusted Jesus Christ for your eternal salvation, you've got something far better than Tupperware on your side. You've got God's Holy Spirit!

"In Him, you also, after listening to the message of truth, the Gospel of your salvation—having also believed, you were sealed in Him with the Holy Spirit of promise...." (Ephesians 1:13 NASB)

"...Scripture has locked up everything under the control of sin, so that what was promised, being given through faith in Jesus Christ, might be given to those who believe." (Galatians 3:22 NIV)

"And may the God of peace himself sanctify you in all things; that your whole spirit, and soul, and body, may be preserved blameless in the coming of our Lord Jesus Christ. He is faithful who hath called you, who also will do it." (1 Thessalonians 5:23-24 Douay-Rheims Bible)

"They will still bear fruit in old age, they will stay fresh...." (Psalm 92:14 NIV)

Salvation is God's Divine Tupperware!

What Never Gets Reduced?

In today's economy it's important to stretch every dollar. So, if you're like us, when shopping for food and other household items, you try to be thrifty. We take advantage of advertised specials and try to stock up on the things we frequently use

REDUCED FOR QUICK SALE

when they're on sale. We also redeem coupons. But we save the most money by shopping at the "Reduced" section of our local supermarket. We find canned and boxed goods, bakery items and meats, at almost half off the regular retail price. Why are these items marked down so much?

Most of these items are damaged. Or rather the outer packaging is damaged. Boxes tend to get battered during shipping. Cans suffer dents and dings. Baked goods such as sliced bread can get a little *smushed*—probably from shoppers squeezing the loaves to check for freshness. Cakes and pies sometime crumble about the edges. Apples and oranges pick up a bruise or two from being jostled about and bumped by other fruit. Meats go from crimson to dull brown, because after sitting a couple days under the bright fluorescent lights, the food coloring they're injected with starts to fade. Really, instead of calling it the "Reduced Items" section, the manager could rename it the "Damaged Goods" section.

Now mind you, there's nothing actually wrong with these items. The bruised fruit is just as fresh and nourishing as the unbruised. The boxes and cans no longer have that "perfect" appearance, either, but the food inside is just as tasty. The meats may look too old, but they're not. And the baked goods may look like they've been knocked around a bit, but they're still delicious! So why are they reduced? Because these items look a little worse for wear, a little beat, many people don't want them. Others will accept them but—because they view these "slightly damaged" items as "second best"—only if the price is right. There's nothing wrong with these goods, but shoppers have nonetheless devalued them.

Okay, why'd we write three long paragraphs about reduced groceries? To make a point: many of us today may be feeling like "damaged goods"! True, life has a way of dealing some blows; we start collecting "dings" and "dents." We get battered by circumstances, bruised by our mistakes and failures. We get smushed when others try to squeeze us into doing things their way. We get categorized as being too old, too young, or too something. We may be feeling a bit crumbled about the edges, and a little beat. Maybe we're feeling like we're second best, because some not-very-savvy people have devalued us.

We don't need to feel this way. Our "packaging" may look a little worse for wear, but in God's economy each and every one of us is priceless! Some of us may have failed in marriage or business; some of us may be dealing with a wayward child, or battling an addiction. ALL of us have made mistakes. But God doesn't relegate us to a "reduced value" section. In society we may *look* like damaged goods, but we are *not!* God sees beyond our less than perfect lives. He sees the potential inside each of us. Which is why He gives us all a second chance —and a third, and a fourth, and a fifth, and you get the point.

God's "mercy endures forever"! (1 Chronicles 16:34 GWT) "...His lovingkindness is everlasting"! (Psalm 136:26 NASB)

"Don't judge by... appearance.... The LORD doesn't see things the way you see them. People judge by outward appearance, but the LORD looks at the heart." (1 Samuel 16:7 NLT)

You make mistakes, but you are not a mistake! You may have failed, but you're not a failure! You may have lost, but you're not a loser! Thank God, we don't need to be perfect to please our Heavenly Father. We just need to be faithful. (Matthew 25:21)

A Place at the Table

We enjoy having guests over for lunch or dinner and, in anticipation of our guests, we usually decorate the table with a theme. One of our favorite themes is songbirds. So our guests tend to be greeted by a table adorned with dinnerware embellished with cardinals, chickadees and goldfinches, along with color-coordinated placemats and tiny birds that are actually place-card holders—each one proudly displaying the name of an honored guest. We're not trying to be "fancy"; we're trying to make our guests feel special. And when they see the preparations, and their names displayed, their faces light up with big smiles.

Place cards and place-card holders date back to Edwardian times but were popularized during the Victorian Era. Place cards served several purposes: in earlier days, social ranking was important to people—not like today, we hope!—and people were seated in order of their ranking, which was based on age, economics and other factors affecting social standing, such as military or civil positions. *Ahem*, yes, quite so!

Place cards were also used to ensure guests were suitably matched to a person of similar temperament and interests, hence promoting social interaction and ensuring no one felt uncomfortable or got left out of a conversation. We fully approve of this particular use of place cards, because in general, we go out of our way to make each guest feel at home and to involve them in easy conversation.

A third use of place cards was a bit more devious, and it involved the romantic schemes of the hostess, who imagined that single male guest "A" would really hit it off with unmarried female guest "B"! The matchmaking intentions of the hostess no doubt being a nice wedding to attend, followed by christenings for future children "C" through "F"! We would never stoop to such shenanigans. At least, we'd never confess to it.

But really, our personal reasons for having place cards is solely to make our guests feel welcome and extra special. Imagine, you walk to a table covered with cheery decorations, and next to one of the place settings is a card with your name inscribed upon it. What do you think? Our hope is that you would immediately realize several things: first, that you were purposely invited—you're not an afterthought, a last minute addition, just someone we allowed to pull up a chair.

We want you to know we intended for you to be here. It was always in our plans to have you dining at our table. And because it was always in our plans, we made special preparations just for you! When you see your place card, you realize we have a seat picked out just for you, a special place reserved for you and *no one else* is going to take. *It. Has. Your. Name. On it!*

And guess what?

Heaven is like a big dining table with place cards. "Blessed are those who are invited to the lamb's wedding banquet.'" (Revelation 19:9 GWT) Each "place card" has the name of a special guest God has invited to dine with Him. These names also appear on His guest list, "written in the Lamb's book of life..." (Revelation 13:8 NIV)

Our Heavenly Father wants us to feel welcome. He wants us to know that we're not an afterthought; we were always in His plans. God made special arrangements for each of us. He wants us to realize that He has set aside a special place for each of us. We have a reserved seat in His kingdom, a special chair at His table—a spot with our name on it!

"If I go and prepare a place for you, I will come again and receive you to Myself, that where I am, there you may be also." (John 14:3 NASB)

We hope you're on God's guest list; that He's inscribed your name on a place card. Of course, you have to let the Lord know you're ready to attend—by allowing Jesus Christ to redeem you. (And we all need redemption!)

For God loved the world so much that he gave His one and only Son, so that everyone who believes in Him will not perish but have eternal life. —John 3:16 NLT

Easy Open!

There's a funny comedy sketch from the old *Carol Burnett Show*, in which Carol's character enters her kitchen with several bags of groceries. She's hungry and she's looking forward to snacking on some of the treats she just purchased. Unfortunately, she can't get any of the bags, boxes, or cans open! Over the next 5 minutes, she struggles in vain to get into various packages, and toward the end succeeds only in opening a gash in her thumb! She hurries to apply a Band-Aid, but...she can't get into the protective, sterile wrapper!

CBS Television

Have you ever experienced anything like this? We have. That is, *one* of us frequently struggles with opening kitchen items! Yes, one of us is ... "container challenged!" A bottle of cola? We need a pair of pliers to unscrew the top! A bag of chips: we need heavy-duty kitchen shears. And you know those wide-mouthed caps that come on those huge plastic bottles of laundry detergent—the caps that double as "wash load" measuring cups? We still haven't quite figured out that one!

Once, we got this plastic tub of little frozen cream puffs, and we had to read the opening instructions three times before we figured out what the manufacture was telling us. We located this nearly imperceptible indentation along the edge of the container, and (according to the label) needed to gently pry up near this indentation in order to "break loose" a tab. Once the tab broke loose, all we had to do was lift the lid at that corner. One big problem: we couldn't get the plastic to break! We had to go to the garage and get a screwdriver, and then spent several aggravating moments digging and twisting into the edge of the plastic lid. Maybe the real "cream puffs" were outside the box!

Sometimes we wonder if the engineers who design these cans, bottles, boxes and bags aren't enjoying a private little joke at our expense. Then we remind ourselves that consumer goods are supposed to be hard to open—and there's good reasons why! Manufacturers want to protect their consumers, for one. They don't want shoppers easily opening a can of mixed nuts in the aisle at Walmart to see if they're salty enough to suit their tastes—or to simply satisfy a sudden snack attack—and then putting the container back on the shelf. Manufacturers want to protect their products from being consumed, contaminated, pilfered, and possibly even poisoned! (Yes, that actually happened a few decades ago.)

Furthermore, cleaning fluids and over-the-counter drugs labeled as "childproof" need to be just that: impervious to the curiosity and tenacity of industrious little kids! The downside of "safe and secure" packaging is that it makes it really tough for some of us to get into a bag of cookies or a box of crackers! We're all for safety, but does everything have to be so hard to get into?!?!

Well, not *everything* in life is hard to get into. In fact, there's at least two things we can think of, that were actually designed to be easy to get into: the Family of God and, by extension, the Kingdom of Heaven. These two things aren't even childproof! Jesus said, "...Unless you change and become like little children, you will never enter the Kingdom of Heaven." (Matthew 18:3 Berean Study Bible)

The instructions for getting into God's Family are easy to follow. It's all outlined in the Word of God—and our Heavenly Father even made getting into His Word easy! The Gospel of Salvation through Christ is simple enough that even a child can understand it, because God wants everyone to have easy access to Him.

We may have trouble opening a can of spam, but opening our Bibles is a breeze! We may have trouble getting into a bag of chips, but getting into God's Spiritual Family is a cinch: "But as many as received Him, to them He gave the right to become children of God, even to those who believe in His name...." (John 1:12 NASB)

Want God to open the way for you? Just follow these "EASY OPEN" instructions:

If you confess with your mouth that Jesus is Lord
and believe in your heart that God raised him
from the dead, you will be saved...
—Roman 10:9 NLT

Something Fishy!

Any of this sound familiar? "He's a good catch"; "That story had me hooked from the very first sentence"; "She's not the only fish in the ocean"; "I'll let you off the hook." There are numerous expressions that liken people to fish. It's a good analogy because we have a lot in common with our finny friends. Think about some of the people you know: there are "puffer fish" who like to boast, eels who are downright slimy, and even the occasional shark we have to watch out for. Some of us may feel like we've reached the big ocean, while some of us feel like we're living in a fishbowl. Some of us benefit every day from life in a "freshwater" environment, while some of us may be floundering in a dirty pool.

Jesus Christ was the first to liken people to fish. He told His disciples, "Follow Me, and I will make you fishers of men." (Matthew 4:19 NASB) His use of the analogy demonstrates how well the Lord understands us: fish tend to do their own thing, and catching one can be very difficult. That describes us all. Furthermore, a good fisherman must hook or net a fish just as he finds it—slippery and scaly, thrashing and splashing; it's only after he lands it that he begins to clean it. And he definitely needs to clean it, because fish, left the way they naturally exist, are always a little smelly. The process perfectly describes what Christ does: He receives each of us just as we are, but because of His Love for us, because of His desire that each of us become the best we can be, He "cleans" everyone He catches. And, you guessed it, cleaning *us* is not much different from cleaning a fish!

Here's the first step in the process necessary to prepare a "fish" for the table of life.

A good cook does several things to make a fish appealing, appetizing, and flavorful; but first, the fish needs to be *washed.* The Bible teaches us that we "fish" can be washed by the blood of the lamb. (Hebrews 10:22 NLT; Revelation 7:14) This is the blood Christ shed when he was crucified. The blood, once we accept Christ as personal Lord and Savior, cleanses us of all unrighteousness, including our past mistakes, and the guilt that often accompanies them—all that pond scum that makes us smell and holds us back in life. "But if we walk in the light, as God is in the light, then we have fellowship with each other, and the blood of Jesus, His son, cleanses us from all sin." (1 John 1:7 NLT)

Smelling a bit fishy today? Have you been floundering in a dirty tank? Are you swimming wherever the currents carry you? Before we discuss the next step in preparing a fish, we'd like to invite you to swim into the net of Jesus Christ; to stop treading water and jump into the boat. (We promise no one will try to serve you up for dinner!) If you want to swim with the rest of us, then read Romans 10:9 and follow the directions.

Cleaning Fish
(Preparing a Fish for the Table #1)

By using the analogy of fishing, Jesus Christ demonstrated how well He understands us: like fish, people tend to do their own thing and catching one can be difficult. And, our Savior, like a good fisherman, hooks or nets us just as we are: slippery, sometimes slimy, and always stinky—just like real fish!

After all, you can't clean a fish *before* you catch it! So Christ receives each of us just as we are, with all our faults, all our baggage. But because He wants us to become the best we can be, He "cleans" everyone He catches. And, cleaning us is not much different from cleaning a fish!

After washing, the next step in preparing a fish for the table of life is to CUT OFF THE HEAD! *Yikes!* But it's not as bad as it sounds. The head represents the mind, and specifically, how we think and what we think. And, as Gautama Siddharta, the founder of Buddhism stated, "The mind is everything; what you think, you become." Of course, there's some skepticism as to whether Buddha actually did say this; but if he did, he was simply restating one of our favorite Bible verses, written at least two centuries before Buddha was born: "As [a man] thinketh in his heart, so is he" (Proverbs 23:7 KJV)

So apparently, it's not the clothes that make the man, but rather his thoughts. (Or her thoughts; we're certainly not chauvinistic.) And, unlike that credit card commercial that asks, "What's in your wallet?" the more pressing question is, what's in your head? *Wait, don't answer that!*

Let's return to cleaning a fish. Imagine: the catch of the day is lying there on your cutting board, that blank expression, that gaping mouth that doesn't say anything, that cold, dead eye staring back at you. *Yuck.* No one at your table will want to see that, so the first thing you do is remove the head. Well, God sort of does the same with each of us. Not literally,

Hey, do you really want fish tonight? It's not even Friday... and I'm loaded with mercury... and there's a sale on chicken this week... and you didn't ask me if I have any last requests! Changed your mind yet? No? You sure? Uh, could I be blindfolded, please? I'd rather not see what happens next.

of course, but He gives us something far more pleasing, "the mind of Christ" (1 Corinthians 2:16), transforming our lifeless (fishy) countenances.

God puts the sparkle of hope into our "dead" eyes; and we go from "gaping and speechless" to the sudden realization that God has given us a hope and a future and a purpose. Each of us goes from being just a helpless creature on the cutting board of life, to becoming a wonderful and beneficial "new creation."

"This means that anyone who belongs to Christ has become a new person. The old life is gone; a new life has begun! (2 Corinthians 5:17 NLT)

Can Jesus Christ cook, or can He COOK? He takes someone with a fishy past and transforms him or her into the pièce de résistance! Gourmet all the way!

A Fish Out of Water
(Preparing a Fish for the Table #2)

We've been using the analogy of fish and fishing to describe our relationship with Christ: first, we swim into His net, just as we are (a bit fishy); afterwards, Christ begins to clean us like a fisherman cleans his prize catch.

First, the fish's head needs to be removed. *Cut off the head?* For a fish, literally; for us, figuratively. For us, the head represents our thoughts and our perspective. As far as our perspective of life, we need to start seeing our lives, other people and all things, as God sees them. We must adopt a Judeo-Christian worldview; stop thinking the way the secular world thinks and start thinking the way God desires us. For instance, this world teaches that we need to look a certain way, dress a certain way, act a certain way, have a certain amount of money and move in certain social circles; and some people think that to truly have value, we need to be a certain color, or a certain gender, or belong to a certain fraternity, club, denomination, church … we could go on and on.

But what does God think? On the value of each of us, God wants you to be able to declare: "Thank You (God) for making me so wonderfully complex! Your workmanship is marvelous—how well I know it! (Psalm 139:14 NLT) But exactly how will we know it? On acceptance, God declares: "Therefore, accept each other just as Christ has accepted you so that God will be given glory." (Romans 15:7 NLT)

Again, how can we know such awesome things? We won't unless we dive into the Word of God. And *dive* is the perfect word for us *fishes*, because the Holy Scriptures are frequently compared to water. Water cleanses, refreshes, and sustains us, just like God's Word—if we let it! Which takes us back to the head: are we allowing God to cleanse our thoughts by "washing with water through the word"? (Ephesians 5:26 NIV) The Bible teaches that after we come to Christ we must renew (reprogram, refresh, and replenish) our minds daily!

This is a neverending process. Medical doctors state that, in order to be healthy, we need to drink a sufficient amount of water each day. Similarly, to keep our sanity in this crazy, competitive, often chaotic great big world of ours, we need to daily flush out our "stinking thinking" (doubt, fear, hatred, selfishness, and all the other negative thoughts that normally and naturally swim in our heads) with positive, faith-filled thoughts. Easy, right? No way! We're constantly bombarded with negative thoughts, from the things we read, hear, and see. Flushing out the bad stuff takes a steady flow of the good stuff, the water of the Word. Read it and ruminate on it, remember it and remind yourself of it.

"And now, dear brothers and sisters, one final thing. Fix your thoughts on what is true, and honorable, and right, and pure, and lovely, and admirable. Think about things that are excellent and worthy of praise." (Philippians 4:8 NLT)

Here's another way of putting it: "Don't become like the people of this world. [pessimistic, cruel, critical, spiteful, etc.]

Instead, change the way you think. Then you will always be able to determine what God really wants—what is good, pleasing, and perfect." (Romans 12:2 GWT)

Swim in the Word of God. Frolic and bathe in it! Lest you become like a fish out of water!

Get Rid of the Tail!
(Preparing a Fish for the Table #3)

The tail of a fish is boney, scaly, hard to chew and not very flavorful. When preparing a fish, it pays to get rid of it. Christ wants to do the same when He's preparing His "fish" for the table of life.

In nature the tail of a fish performs two very important tasks: it propels and steers. It allows our finny friends to swim wherever they wish and whenever they wish. We, too, have something that enables us to go where we want when we want. It's called the human will. The human will motivates and empowers us. It gives direction and determination. The phrases "He (or she) has a lot of will power" and "Where there's a will there's a way" spring to mind. And when someone is stubborn, we often describe the person as "strong-willed."

The Good, the Bad, and the Ugly: God created each of us to have a will of our own—the ability to choose for ourselves, to swim in our own personal style. When He first created us, He looked down and declared, *that's good!* And although He hopes we'll use this God-given freedom to make the right decisions in life—*for instance, to swim beside Him, not away from Him; in His great ocean, not in a mud puddle*—we don't often choose the best course for ourselves.

That's bad! In fact, without God's daily guidance in every area of life, we always manage to screw things up. That's when things can get pretty ugly! But that's okay. God understands that we're only human. Again, He created us that way. He could have made us to be like little windup robots, but He didn't want that. He wanted us to have free will.

So how do we reconcile our free will (our desires, our plans, our inclinations, our dispositions, and our always poor choices) with God's better plan and direction for our lives? Simple, make a conscious decision every day to "get rid of the tail"; to surrender your will and choose to do His will; to do the things He wants, not the things you want; to swim with God, *with* the current and not against it.

In the end (*haha*, remember the fish's tail?), it all comes down to the choices we make because, after all, we have a free will. We can swim our way or swim with God, following Him wherever He leads.

> *Jesus said..."If any of you wants to be my follower,*
> *you must turn from your selfish ways,*
> *take up your cross, and follow me."*
> —Matthew 16:24 NLT

Surfin' Safari
(Preparing a Fish for the Table #4)

Remember that old hit song by the Beach Boys?

Let's go surfin' now,
Everybody's learning how.
Come on and safari with me!

Excellent! Now hold that thought. We've been using the analogy of fish and fishing to describe our relationship with Christ: first, we swim into His net, just as we are (a bit fishy); afterwards, Christ begins to clean us like a fisherman cleans his prize catch, and then there are steps we should take which prepare us for the table of life.

We previously discussed getting rid of the tail! A fish's tail performs two very important tasks: it propels and steers, allowing our finny friends to swim wherever they wish. We, too, have something that enables us to go wherever we want, whenever we want, to do whatever we want. It's called the free will. It's a nice little trait God created in us, because He wanted us to have the freedom to make our own choices. Only one problem: when we start calling the shots, when we do things our way, we generally make a royal mess of it! That's why God hopes we'll get rid of the "tail" by making a conscious effort to surrender our will and choose to do His will; to do the things He wants, not the things you want; to swim with God, not away from Him!

Swimming with God is just like going on a Surfin' Safari! Seriously! First, there's always a leader in these ventures, and yup, you guessed it, that would be Jesus Christ.

Second, what's a safari without a map? Not to worry, we got one of those, too; and it outlines all the best spots for our adventure and shows us exactly how to get there. Our map is the Word of God: "Your Word is a lamp to my feet and a light to my path." (Psalm 119:105 NASB) Precisely what a good map should be! In fact, the Bible teaches us how to navigate the often treacherous waters of life; to steer away from the shallows and avoid running aground.

But even with the best map in hand, it's still comforting to have a savvy, resourceful guide along with us. So, thirdly, we've contracted with the world's greatest safari guide—the Holy Spirit. Jesus promised us that "the Comforter, who is the Holy Spirit, whom the Father will send in my name, he shall teach you all things...." (John 14:26 KJ2000) and "will guide you into all truth." (John 16:13 NLT)

Why not start swimming with Christ today? Pull out God's navigational charts and start listening to the Holy Guide. "Come on and safari with me!"

You've Got Guts!
(Preparing a Fish for the Table #5)

You've Got Guts! If someone like John Wayne said that to you, you could take it as a real compliment; but when the Bible states it ... well, not so much. We'll explain why in a moment.

When preparing a fish for your family, you usually want to cut off the head and tail. Those things don't look too appetizing on the plate. One thing you'll always want to do, though, is to make a slit down the fish's belly and remove all the guts: the stomach and the intestines. If you don't, when you sit down to eat, you won't be having just fish for dinner; you'll also be having everything your finny friend was having before you reeled him in. That's right. You'll be eating the contents of the fish's stomach along with the—*ahem*—stuff in the fish's intestines. *Yech!* That's not very appealing.

Well, when God prepares each us for a new life with Him, He also wants to get rid of our guts. No, He doesn't want to remove our vital organs—this is not Dr. Frankenstein's Lab Class. But we can liken our "guts" to our natural, "fleshly" appetites and inclinations—and those things are not appealing to God. Why? Because our natural inclinations always lead us to do the wrong thing. Ever hear the expression "My gut reaction"? Follow your gut, and you might be inclined to do something you'd later regret, like punching that obnoxious co-worker in the snout. (Yes, yes, we know he's been asking for it, but you mustn't give in to your gut feelings.)

In addition to the sometimes savage, usually impulsive, inclinations of your gut, there also are equally savage appetites (cravings) that lead us to make impulsive choices. We'll rush into a bad relationship without taking the time to think things through; we'll charge a new outfit that's on sale, or drop several bills on a cool entertainment gadget, without truly counting the cost of how we'll afford it; and without giving a single thought to calories or how we'll fit into the new jeans we bought last month, we'll scarf down a whole pint of Ben & Jerry's—after we've polished off a large Domino's pizza! Face it, our appetites can and often do control us.

Speaking of the appetite, ever pass a McDonald's and decide you're about to have a Mac Attack? You may not even

feel hungry until you spy those golden arches, but suddenly you swerve across two lanes of traffic and bounce over a curb for a pack of fries! Are you weird? No. There's even a story in the Bible that illustrates the power of the appetite:

In Genesis chapter 25, Esau, the firstborn son of Isaac, and his father's favorite, was in line to inherit the lion's share of Isaac's estate and authority.

Esau was to receive not simply an inheritance, but also Isaac's position, power and prominence. This was his birthright as the firstborn son. It was his whole future ... and he gave it all away in return for a bowl of stew! Yes, he sold his life for a bunch of beans. Hard to believe? But wait, that's not all, folks: Esau wasn't malnourished; nor had he gone days without a meal. He simply had a huge appetite and didn't have enough discipline to say no to his stomach (his gut). No doubt, long after that meal became just another outdoor memory, Esau regretted his poor judgment and rash decision. Poor guy was just a victim of a kosher Mac Attack!

Now, before any of our readers declare that food is not their problem, let's point out that our appetites (our gut inclinations and cravings) take many forms. We may crave position, power, fame, fortune, *things* (you know, grown up toys), and even sex. (Hard to believe that last one, right?) In and of themselves, such things are not bad, nor is craving them a horrible thing.

These are our natural inclinations and appetites, our gut feelings; what's bad is when we allow ourselves to be controlled by our appetites; When we eat so much sugar that we develop diabetes, or shop so much that we go in debt, or work so much to climb the ladder of success that we neglect and even risk losing our loved ones; or we ... well, we'll leave the last one to your imagination. Feeding our appetites may bring us temporary satisfaction, but it always comes at a price: our health, our freedom, our peace of mind, even our own self-respect.

Christ has a better plan for His fishes. He doesn't want us controlled by our appetites; making decisions we'll later regret (like Esau); shackled to our gut desires. Instead, He wants us to scoop out the guts. That's how we prepare a fish, and it's how we prepare ourselves to lead healthy, productive, fulfilled lives without regrets, excessive debts, shackles or bonds. Scoop out the gut inclinations and appetites by asking God to help you live a disciplined life. Seek to do His will, not yours. Don't be led by the things you want and crave, be led by God's Word instead. Don't buy in to that old Burger King ad to "Have it your way"; have it God's way! In the long run, you'll find it tastier, more ful*filling*, and more nourishing. And you won't need to buy larger jeans.

Take control: "Don't you realize that your body is the temple of the Holy Spirit, who lives in you and was given to you by God? You do not belong to yourself." (1 Corinthians 6:19 NLT) Therefore, "...Let the Holy Spirit guide your lives. Then you won't be doing what your sinful nature craves." (Galatians 5:16 NLT)

Give It a Rest!

Good cooks agree: we may not tire of food, but food gets tired. Apparently.

Wine connoisseurs admonish us that when we open a bottle of wine we should "let it breathe" before serving it. Okay. After all, the bottle was airtight, so the wine must have been suffocating in there.

And when we remove a bird or a roast from the oven, the recipes always state, "Let it rest!" Why should we? We did all the work cooking the piece of meat. And now we're hungry!

We actually know the reason for this one: As meat cooks, the natural moisture inside is pushed outward. This moisture migrates toward the surface of the meat. Some of it eventually evaporates. The remaining moisture is concentrated near the surface. When you take a roast or bird from the oven, the cooked meat needs to "rest," thereby allowing sufficient time for the remaining moisture (the juices) to evenly redistribute throughout the meat.

If you cut into the meat right away, those juices—concentrated near the surface—will pool and drain off, and your beautiful turkey or slaved-over roast will end up being very dry.

141

Letting meat rest allows it to re-absorb the juices that keep it tender. And, guess what? People are just like roasted meat—or turkeys, if you prefer. *Ahem*, please read on.

In addition to *Angel in the Kitchen,* we have two other series. In *Diet for Dreamers* and *Encouragement for Creators,* we try to inspire people to set goals and achieve them. And we all need goals, something to shoot for, in order to be healthy and happy. But sometimes we get too caught up in chasing our dreams, too focused on our ambitions, that we lose sight of all the wonderful things in this world that make life so special to begin with. So, after cooking up plans for the future, we need to let them rest. If we don't, we just might find ourselves getting a little dry spiritually, and our hearts not quite as tender.

We can sell our souls to our jobs, projects, dreams, and even ministries—to the point where we have no time for friends and family; no time to stop, think, catch our breath, and smell the proverbial roses. People climbing the corporate ladder may neglect (and possibly lose) their loved ones in a mad dash to make it to the top. Dreamers often wear themselves out, and often get depressed, trying to make their wishes come true while holding down demanding day jobs. People in ministry, including pastors, priests, and rabbis, often get burned out for the world's greatest mission in life.

—All because they failed to periodically take a break and spend time replenishing. Like the recipe states, "Let it rest!"

Nothing is worth the price of fatigue and depression, not to mention any broken relationships. These "ailments" can ultimately derail the very dreams and ministries that caused them. Stay focused, stay committed, but also take some time off. Rest and recreation (focusing on something else for a time—such as family) are antidotes to depression and exhaustion. And retreating and recharging with God and His Word are vital for preventing burnout.

He maketh me to lie down in green pastures.
Psalm 23:2

Our Heavenly Father was the first to set the example for us to follow. After creating the Universe in 6 days, He rested from His work on the seventh. And when He walked the earth, Jesus Christ the Lord frequently retreated so He could recharge. He also rested and He indulged in recreation (food and fellowship)—and His mission, His dream and His goal were far more important than anything we've been up to!

God went even further: He established the seventh day —the Sabbath—as the official day for retreating, resting, recharging and recreating! (See Exodus 34:21) You see, He knows we have this bad habit of striving, competing, obsessing, and getting caught up in the moment. God the "Master Chef" is admonishing us to "let it rest"! He wants us to be "juicy" with the Spirit of God, refreshed with His holy Word, and tenderhearted toward our friends and families; not tough and all dried out.

Got a dream, a goal, a job or a ministry? Of course you do. But every so often, you need to give it a rest! Take time to recharge. "Come to me, all of you who are weary and loaded down with burdens, and I will give you rest." (Matthew 11:28 ISV)

New Seasons Ahead

Deep snow in winter, tall grain in summer.
—Estonian proverb

After a long winter, the arrival of spring brings a welcome change of pace. Despite the often annoyingly accurate weather predictions of a certain grumpy groundhog, spring officially starts on March 20;

and we always get excited over the prospects of longer days and milder temperatures! We love the change of seasons. As the weather changes, so do our wardrobe and activities. With warmer months ahead we begin to store away our sweaters and long sleeves, and move our summer outfits to the front of the closet.

We marvel at the changes taking place in nature, too. With spring, all of life seems renewed. In the woods surrounding Woodhaven, the trees thicken with vibrant green leaves, the landscape becomes speckled with the blossoms of dogwoods and mountain laurel. Our old friends the hummingbirds return, rejoining our year-round regulars: cardinals, goldfinches, chickadees, huge pileated woodpeckers, and even a red hawk.

Along with the change of seasons, come changes in what we tend to eat. All those hearty soups and stews that warmed us during the winter no longer have as much appeal. Our tastes turn away from turkeys and roasts, to grilled steaks and fresh vegetables. We start craving cool crisp salads and other, lighter fare.

Our desserts change, too. In the winter we love warm bread pudding in brandy sauce, and hot apple pie. Now, we're ready to serve and enjoy lots of ice cream. One of our favorite warm-weather desserts is homemade vanilla ice cream topped with fresh, sliced strawberries. We like to serve it up in a pretty margarita glass and add a dollop of whipped cream!

Can you think of other tasty seasonal foods? How about pumpkin pie and eggnog for fall and winter? Deviled eggs and Challah bread during spring? Hotdogs and watermelon during summer? These are a few of our favorites, but you probably can list many others.

Just as there are seasons of the year—accompanied by seasonal foods and seasonal clothes—there also are seasons of life. Seasons of sowing and reaping, of adversity and rest. King Solomon wrote, "For everything there is a season, a time for every activity under heaven. ...A time to cry and a time to laugh. A time to grieve and a time to dance. ...Yet God has made everything beautiful for its own time." (Ecclesiastes 3:1, 4 & 11 NLT)

Many of us have gone through seasons of struggles, challenges, grief, and discouragement. Periods in life when it felt like every time we took one step forward, we took two steps back! But, like the weather and our food preferences, these seasons do change. Nothing lasts forever except God's eternal love.

So, no matter what adversity you're facing, "this too shall pass"! Therefore, "...let us not grow weary of doing good, for in due season we will reap, if we do not give up." (Galatians 6:9 ESV)

Don't give up! Keep believing, keep dreaming, keep on doing your best; keep on loving and helping others, and your breakthrough will come!

Are things looking bleak at the moment? Are you going through a "cold, dark season"? Look back at the other times in your life, when you were facing a difficult situation, when you felt like you were at the end of your rope. Those were dark seasons, too—but you're still standing! You came through the tough times, and into a new season. "...The winter is past... Flowers appear on the earth; the season of singing has come...." (Song of Solomon 2:11-12 NIV)

You give [us] peace and quiet from times of trouble....
—Psalm 94:13 GWT

You're Not Butter!

Anyone remember those amusing TV commercials for Parkay margarine? In every Parkay commercial, whenever someone lifted the lid, the yellow tub of margarine would debate its identity. The consumer would argue with the yellow stuff in the container, proclaiming it to be "Parkay!" But Parkay's rejoinder was always the same: "Butter!"

After the consumer tastes the margarine, he or she would nod, agree that Parkay was smooth and creamy, so it must be true: it IS butter. But hey, just because something looks like butter, even tastes like butter, does not necessarily mean it is butter. Butter is butter! Made by contented cows with big brown eyes. Margarine, on the other hand, is a synthetic mixture engineered in a laboratory to approximate the qualities of the real deal. Personally, we'd rather put our trust in cows, not chemists!

All this, however, is beside the point. In these Parkay commercials, that poor yellow tub of margarine had an identity crisis. It wanted to be viewed as butter! Did it really believe it was butter? Nope. At the end of each TV spot, once the consumer gave in and agreed it was butter, the obstinate little yellow tub would tauntingly purr, "Parkay."

Humor us for a moment. What was Parkay's problem? It knew it was margarine and not butter. Yet it wanted to be considered butter. *Aha!* Deep down, Parkay was feeling a little inferior. It wasn't, after all, the real deal. But then, only butter is the genuine article. Does this make Parkay inferior? Does Parkay serve a special purpose in people's diets? Have we totally lost our minds?

There are countless people in society who suffer a

similar identity crisis. Like Parkay, they feel a little inferior to someone else. They go around competing with their friends, family, coworkers—and stubbornly try to convince the world they're someone they're not. Each of these people are unique in their own special way. And, like Parkay, they were created to fill a role only they themselves can fill. And yet, like the poor little tub of margarine, they're not comfortable with who they are. Why?

For many people, their identity is tied to external factors; and they wrongly base their self-worth or significance on their accomplishments, associations, and possessions. Let's briefly examine these factors. *Identity and self-worth have nothing to do with:*

1) What we do. Jobs, career positions, sports, academic achievements, hobbies, and even ministries do not define us. What happens if (when) these functions are taken away? Do we lose our significance? Not in God's eyes: "Before I formed you in the womb I knew you, before you were born I set you apart...." (Jeremiah 1:5 NIV)

2) Nor what we have. Owning stuff seems to confer status in our materialistic society. But big houses, fancy cars, and lots of "toys" can never really satisfy the inner longings we have. To quote the old Beatles song, "Money can't buy me love." Each of us has a God-sized hole in our spirits and no amount of stuff can fill it—only our Lord can do that! "For we are God's masterpiece. He has created us anew in Christ Jesus, so we can do the good things he planned for us long ago." (Ephesians 2:10 NLT) "And what do you benefit if you gain the whole world but lose your own soul? Is anything worth more than your soul?" (Matthew 16:26 NLT)

3) Nor is our worth based on social standards or the opinions of the "in crowd." All that matters is what God has to say about us in His Word. His standards are what we're measured by: "I will give thanks to You, for I am fearfully and wonderfully made; Wonderful are Your works, And my soul knows it very well." (Psalm 139:14 NASB) Furthermore, "...God does not show favoritism." (Romans 2:11 NLT) "...God loved the world

so much that he gave his one and only Son, so that everyone who believes in him will not perish but have eternal life." (John 3:16 NLT)

Friends, we don't have to compare or compete with anyone. We each have infinite value—we're each worth the death of God's only Son, Jesus Christ! We each were placed on this planet by God's design ... and in His wisdom. He doesn't make mistakes. Be the person God made you to be. Be confident in His love and acceptance. Find significance in Him, the Creator of the Universe, and in His plan for your life. It's not WHAT you do that counts, it's the "WHY" that's important!

Remember: you're not butter, you're better!

> ...*Whatsoever you do, do all to the glory of God.*
> —1 Corinthians 10:31 KJ2000

The Cheese Stands Alone!

A couple weeks ago we made a huge dish of baked ziti, which (for those poor souls who've been *culinarily* deprived) is similar to lasagna—layers of noodles, marinated ground beef, and different cheeses. We took it to a friend's house to share, and it was absolutely delicious! Wish you could've had some.

We were tired when we got home, so we did the cook's equivalent of that old housekeeper's trick, "sweeping the dirt under the carpet." Well, it's not *that* bad. We decided to wash the messy Pyrex baking dish in the morning—after we slept on it, so to speak. And we stuck the dish into the oven, where we wouldn't have to look at it. Bad move!

Who wants to wake up to a messy dish in the sink? Not us, which is why we hid it. Honest, we were going to wash it the first thing when we got up the next morning. Only we hid it a little too well. "Out of sight, out of mind." We didn't give that dirty dish a second thought! Not the next day, when we were busy writing; nor the next, when we ran errands; nor the day after that, when we ... *well,* long story short, we didn't use our oven for days! Sure, we cooked on top the range, but we didn't need to bake anything.

When we finally did open the oven, to look for the pizza pan—*What? You don't store your pizza pan in the oven? Ours won't fit anywhere else!*—we were confronted by that messy baking dish. Sitting there. Alone. In the dark. Sulking. Hardening the cheese and sauce of its aching heart ... until all that was left was a dried up, crusted over scab of forgotten ziti. Okay, we're being dramatic. But the cheesy residue of our long-forgotten meal was almost impossible to clean up.

We destroyed our kitchen sponge, using the coarse side of it to scour the dish—and to no affect. That cheese had hardened to cement. A jackhammer wouldn't have been totally out of the question, but we settled on an SOS steel-wool pad and several minutes of hard labor. A just penalty befitting our crime of neglect and forgetfulness. And then—*yuck!*—we needed to toss out the SOS pad!

Hey, don't blame us. We just provide the cheese, God gives the wisdom.

In life, just as with dirty dishes, we all face problems that are much easier to handle when dealt with quickly. Sooner or later, we all manage to make a mess of something, and it's a lot easier to clean our messes when we deal with them immediately. Hiding from an issue, avoiding an unpleasant task, leaving a hurt friend or family member to "harden" while we "sleep on it," only makes the job more difficult—if not impossible to handle.

When dealing with people, never allow angry or harsh words to thicken and crust over, creating a barrier that separates a relationship. After an argument or misunderstanding, work quickly to resolve matters, bring peace, and heal damaged emotions. "I'm sorry" should never be the least used words in your vocabulary! Don't wait until later, either. "Don't go to bed angry." (Ephesians 4:26 GWT) Swallow your pride; for the sake of harmony, humble yourself and seek the person's forgiveness. "...God opposes the proud, but gives grace to the humble." (James 4:6 ESV)

There are far too many cheesy messes in our homes and workplaces, our neighborhoods and houses of worship. And in many cases, we've allowed them to harden. Know what? God wants us to do the dishes no matter how hard we need to scrub. "...If you are presenting a sacrifice at the altar ... and you suddenly remember that someone has something against you, leave your sacrifice there.... Go and be reconciled to that person. Then come and offer your sacrifice to God" (Matthew 5:23-24 NLT)

Take care of your cheesy messes before the job gets tougher. Don't put it off. Don't talk yourself out of it. Things will just get harder. Do it quickly, so both your dishes and your relationships will sparkle.

Spit the Seeds!

We previously stated one of life's cold hard facts: there are *no* perfect foods.

Honey is often called "the perfect food," but honey can be fattening and promote tooth decay. Water is vital to life, but drinking too much water can strip away beneficial electrolytes. Seriously! And although it seems overly critical to complain about the downside of water and various foods, which are otherwise delicious and which have great nutritional value, we usually don't hesitate to approach life with a similar critical eye.

Life, love and relationships will never be perfect! Like food, most aspects of life here on earth are enjoyable and beneficial. Life has great "nutritional" value; but often we focus on the imperfections, the "seeds" in the heart of our relationships, in our jobs, in our places of worship.

Interestingly, we frequently hear friends and coworkers grumbling about life and people, but we rarely if ever hear them complaining about what they're eating. Probably because most of us tend to expect more from life, love, and relationships, than we do from what we eat. (Picky eaters aside.) We previously stated one remedy to this: Keep your high expectations, and always hope for the best, but don't put your high (and mighty) expectations on your spouse, your spiritual leaders, your relatives or your friends.

Face it, no one can meet our lofty expectations—including ourselves! None of us are perfect, so why should we expect others to be? And by the way, almost assuredly, at any given moment, we're not living up to someone else's expectations. In other words, somewhere, at some time, we're letting someone down! Oh well. *C'est la vie!* Anyway, don't put your expectations on people. Instead, put your expectations on God. He's perfect, and He'll never let you down.

Another remedy for avoiding disappointment in life? Read on, as we further discuss a favorite topic—FOOD!!

Crab legs: ever notice that people who love them *really* love them? Personally, we've never enjoyed fighting with our food, and crab is one dish that manages to put up a struggle long after its days are over. Sort of like the crab's last-ditch effort to get revenge. But people who love crab legs don't seem to mind, *at all.* Armed with those heavy-duty cracker gizmos, they happily *snap, crack* and *pop* shells until their knuckles are white and their fingertips red—all this work to secure a tiny piece of crab meat.

Onions: these weird pseudo-veggies manage to get around, and often end up being the life of the party. We invite them into our soups and stews, welcome them in our salads and subs. And we usually include them when we're having steaks or burgers. We absolutely adore onions, but dealing with them often makes us cry! But a few tears never stop us from hanging out with onions!

Watermelon: a summertime favorite. Cool, refreshing, and loaded with a gazillion seeds. But the seeds don't seem to bother most people. We doubt they even notice the seeds. They merrily chomp away at huge bites of crisp red fruit, and their dispositions don't change when they encounter a few seeds. They keep smiling and eating, and just spit the seeds— hopefully not in our direction!

Foods aren't perfect. Neither are people. Why can't we deal with the imperfections of life and people in the same manner we deal with hard shells and tears and seeds? Happily, cheerfully, eagerly. Why aren't we willing to work as hard on our relationships as we do on cracking crab legs? Well, we can. It just takes a little willingness, prayer, and God's grace, to penetrate the shells people hide within.

Why do we run from people and relationships after we shed a few tears? Life can be painful. People disappoint and hurt each other constantly. It's a consequence of the imperfection of the human race. But relationships are worth it. We all have strengths and weaknesses. Each of us has something to offer; but we also, by our very nature, come loaded with "seeds": faults, blind spots, bad habits. Since we all have seeds, shouldn't we be willing to overlook them in others? Better yet, why not enjoy the good things we can find in each and every individual; and simply spit the seeds out? It's Food for thought. Think and pray on it.

Make allowance for each other's faults, and forgive anyone who offends you. Remember, the Lord forgave you, so you must forgive others. —Colossians 3:13 NLT

Most important of all, continue to show deep love for each other, for love covers a multitude of sins.
—1 Peter 4:8 NLT

Seeds of Faith

We all have hopes and dreams, visions and goals. But the journey to accomplishing our goals, seeing our dreams fulfilled, or receiving a promise, can take years. Many people start the journey strong, but often, just short of the finish line, they run out of steam and give up.

If we're going to stay on course—and reach our goals—we need to be fueled by faith: an unshakeable belief in the God of Abraham, Isaac and Israel; an abiding trust in His goodness and lovingkindness; and a resolute confidence in His ability and willingness to fulfill His promises. "...Faith is the reality of what is hoped for...." (Hebrews 11:1 Holman CSB) In other words, faith is treating God's promises as a "done deal"—despite our circumstances or any obstacles, and regardless of what other people say.

But how much faith is enough? Jesus said, "...If you have faith the size of a mustard seed, you will say to this mountain, 'Move from here to there,' and it will move; and nothing will be impossible to you." (Matthew 17:20 NASB) To fully understand this verse we return now to the kitchen, that endless source of wisdom and inspiration.

Mustard seeds are among the tiniest in the plant kingdom, usually about one silly millimeter in diameter, or smaller than this asterisk: * (!) And yet, each edible seed is packed with a strong spicy flavor. When properly planted, these small and seemingly insignificant seeds, grow in size and strength, producing the largest of garden plants, with tasty leaves. There are three major types of seeds, black mustard, brown Indian mustard, and white mustard.

When the seeds are ground, the resultant powder is a potent spice that enhances many dishes. The English name mustard is derived from a Latin word meaning burning must. "Must" is the young, unfermented juice of wine grapes, and "burning must" refers to the spicy heat of mustard seeds that have been ground and mixed with a little wine to create a sauce.

Mustard was originally considered a medicinal plant rather than an herb for cooking. In fact, the Greek scientist Pythagoras used mustard as a remedy for scorpion stings, during the sixth century B.C.; and a hundred years later, Hippocrates used it in a variety of medicines and plasters to "cure" toothaches and several other ailments.

But in latter days, mustard was simply used to spice up dishes that needed ... *well* ... spicing up! And it's been called a "food deodorant," also, because it can mask any unpleasant taste of what the cook happens to be dishing out. Pope John XII was so fond of mustard that he created a new Vatican position, Grand mustard-maker to the Pope. He then promptly filled the post with his nephew. (Was this the historical origin of nepotism?)

So, when Jesus spoke of mustard-seed faith, our Lord couldn't have drawn a better comparison: a tiny bit of faith can produce huge results; faith is potent; it can soothe us in times of misery and heartache; it helps us endure the unpleasantness of trials, and "deodorize" any circumstances of life that may stink! When it comes to Faith—just like mustard —a little dab goes a long way.

"But what if I don't have even a little dab of faith?" Yes, you do. You already have plenty of faith: "For by the grace given to me, I tell everyone among you not to think of himself more highly than he should think. Instead, think sensibly, as God has distributed a measure of faith to each one." (Romans 12:3 Holman CSB) Would God ask you to put your faith in Him, without first giving you faith? *Nah!* God has given us everything we need to believe in Him and do his will.

But we must activate our faith: One way we do this is by reading and listening to the Word of God. The historical account of His faithfulness to us, of His mercy and loving-kindness, of His miracles, encourages us and feeds our faith. "...Faith comes by hearing, and hearing by the word of God." (Romans 10:17 KJ2000)

We also encourage our faith by fellowshipping with other believers. "...Encourage one another and build each other up...." (1 Thessalonians 5:11 NIV)

And by talking to God. Yes, we call this prayer, but that's just a fancy word for sharing your thoughts, concerns, and problems with the Lord—in the same way you'd share with a really close friend, someone you totally trust and can confide in. We can trust and confide in our Heavenly Father; we can have total faith in our invisible God. No, we can't see Him, but He's there by our side at all times! (John 15:15) That's faith!

Nothing's Wasted!

We have a friend who's a folk artist. A few years back he carved and painted two small refrigerator magnets that have become prized decorations in our kitchen. One is the Planters mascot, Mister Peanut; the other is the Pillsbury Doughboy, Poppin' Fresh. Both are well made, and our friend absolutely nailed the characters.

Our friend also likes to cook—Southern-style! Once, he said that whenever he boiled potatoes for mashing, he'd drain off the water and save it. The liquid contained a lot of the starch from the spuds, as well as the potato flavor that's currently popular in breads. He'd use this liquid instead of plain water whenever he made biscuits. The biscuits held together better and had a richer flavor!

It's similar to what we do when boiling chicken for certain dishes: we save the broth and use it to flavor soups, casseroles, and our favorite chicken and rice dish. Guests often ask what gives the rice such a savory flavor. We always give the short, direct answer. But the longer, indirect answer is that we don't waste anything; what many people decant, cut away, and cast out—assuming it to be worthless—is always put to good use in our kitchen. Even fruit and vegetable peelings can be composted.

Another item we save and *repurpose* is stale bread. We use it to make stuffing and bread pudding. Why waste a good thing, even if it appears to be "bad"—just like the cloudy liquid left over from boiled potatoes. In the kitchen, *everything* that's seemingly of no value, seemingly a "lost cause" or a "complete waste" can serve a good purpose. Savvy cooks never waste. And neither does God.

The savviest "cook" in the kitchen of life is our Heavenly Father, and He never wastes anything. He simply repurposes it for His use. That means the fallout from a failed relationship or business venture will be put to good use in our lives. God may use a painful or embarrassing experience to teach us a truth, help us develop better character, or get us ready for a bigger challenge. Sometimes, He simply wants to get us on the right track again, so that he can fulfill our special destiny.

He uses defeat to make us stronger. He repurposes grief to make us compassionate. He allows closed doors and missed "opportunities" to keep us out of trouble. He doesn't waste anything.

Whatever we've suffered, whatever we're going through, whatever mistakes we've made, God always finds a good use for these "bad" experiences—which seem at the time like "lost causes"; like a "complete waste"! But in God's kitchen there's no waste. Every tear you've shed, every heartache you've endured, every moment of sorrow and suffering, doubt and despair—He's restructured into something new and more wonderful.

We usually don't know what God is cooking up. Nor can we often see how He'll repurpose something wrong and destructive into something right and renewed. But His Word explains to us that He continually does so. We can trust Him, knowing that our losses, our failures, our sorrows are *never* wasted. He is truly the God who renews, repurposes, restructures and reuses all we are, all we have, and all we've gone through—*the good, the bad, and the ugly.*

...You meant evil against me, but God meant it for good in order to bring about this present result....
—Genesis 50:20 NASB

And we know that God causes everything to work together for the good of those who love God and are called according to His purpose for them.
—Romans 8:28 NLT

Don't miss *Angel in the Kitchen 2*

And join Tom and Wilma for more humor and inspiration at their website, <u>AngelAtTheDoor.com</u>

LIST OF BIBLE TRANSLATIONS CITED

AKJV - *Authorized King James Version,* Cambridge University Press

AMP - *The Amplified Bible*, The Lockman Foundation (2015).

AMPC - *The Amplified Bible: Classic Edition*, Lockman Foundation (1987)

BLB - *Berean Literal Bible*, Bible Hub (2016)

BSB - *Berean Study Bible*, Bible Hub (2016)

CEB - *Common English Bible*, Common English Bible (2011)

CEV - *Contemporary English Version*, American Bible Society (1995)

CJB - David Stern, *Complete Jewish Bible* (1998)

CSB - *Christian Standard Bible*, Holman Bible Publishers (2017)

EHV - *Evangelical Heritage Version*, The Wartburg Project (2017)

ERV - *Easy-to-Read Version*, World Bible Translation Center (2006)

ESV - *The English Standard Version*, Crossway Bibles (2001)

EXB - *The Expanded Bible*, Thomas Nelson Inc. (2011)

GNT - *Good News Translation,* American Bible Society (1992)

GWT - *God's Word*, God's Word to the Nations (1995)

HCSB - *Holman Christian Standard Bible*, Holman Bible Publishers (2003)

ICB - *International Children's Bible*, Thomas Nelson (2015)

ISV - *International Standard Version*, ISV Foundation (1996-2012)

JUB - *Jubilee Bible*, Life Sentence Publishing (2000, 2001, 2010)

KJV - *King James Version* (1611; revised 1769)

KJ21 - *21st Century King James Version,* Deuel Enterprises, Inc. (1994)

MSG - *The Message,* E. H. Peterson (2002)

NASB - *New American Standard Bible*, Lockman Foundation (1995)

NCV - *New Century Version*, Thomas Nelson, Inc. (2005)

NET - *The NET Bible*/New English Trans., Biblical Studies Press (2005)

NIV - *The New International Version*, Biblica, Inc. (1984, 2011)

NKJV - *New King James Version*, Thomas Nelson, Inc. (1982)

NLT - *New Living Translation*, Tyndale House Foundation (1996, 2007)

NOG - *The Names of God Bible*, Baker Publishing Group (2011)

PHILLIPS - J. B. Phillips, *The New Testament in Modern English* (1958)

TLB - *The Living Bible,* Kenneth Taylor (1971)

VOICE - *The Voice Bible,* Thomas Nelson; Ecclesia Bible Society (2012)

WNT - Richard Francis Weymouth, *Weymouth New Testament* (1903)

Notes:

Wilma Espaillat English *grew up in a bilingual, bicultural family in New York and New Jersey, learning firsthand the significance of hospitality in the Hispanic culture. Today she is a published writer, speaker and educator. She has taught a variety of subjects including Business English, Public Speaking, Spanish, and Ancient World History, at both the college and high school levels. She has written high school curriculum for classes in Multicultural Studies, and conducted seminars for civic groups, including law enforcement agencies. She also has taught Bible and Christian Life topics to adults ranging in age from 18 to 80. She is the wife of Tom English.*

Tom English *grew up in a "Southern-fried" family in rural Virginia. Today he is a Senior Chemist at Newport News Shipbuilding. He is also a published writer and award-nominated editor of both fiction and non-fiction. His fantasy-adventure fiction has appeared in print magazines such as* Black Infinity, Weirdbook, *and* All Hallows; *and in several print anthologies, including* Haunted House Short Stories *and* Detective Thrillers Short Stories *(both published in the U.K. by Flame Tree Publishing), and* Gaslight Arcanum: Uncanny Tales of Sherlock Holmes *(Edge SF & Fantasy). Tom also edited the mammoth* Bound for Evil: Curious Tales of Books Gone Bad, *a 2008 Shirley Jackson Award finalist for best anthology. Like his wife, Wilma, he has extensive knowledge in Biblical Studies and has taught many Christian Life classes to singles and "young" married couples ages 18 to 80. He resides with Wilma, surrounded by books and beasts, deep in the woods of New Kent, Virginia.*

Don't miss *ANGEL IN THE KITCHEN 2*

"The Englishes write with style, clarity and gracefulness."
—*The Booklife Prize*

TOM & WILMA'S FAMILY OF ECCENTRIC KITCHEN ANGELS IS BACK!

Meet *Garbo*, our tough-guy garbage pail, the crusty and outspoken *Signor Panini*, and *Mr. Freeze*, star of "The Big Thaw." Learn why *Katie the kettle* frequently shrieks, and discover the curious link between pineapples and hospitality. These are just a few of the "kitchen angels" eagerly waiting to greet you within.

Grab a cup of tea, find a comfy chair, and indulge in a *second* helping of witty and wise articles inspired by food, cooking, and things found in every kitchen: an eccentric ensemble of kitchen angels (Godly messengers) who can teach us important lessons about life, love, relationships, and the world we live in. *Bon appétit!*

ISBN: 978-1732434479 • Softcover • 220 pages

ANGEL IN THE KITCHEN 2

A SECOND HELPING OF
WIT & WISDOM INSPIRED BY FOOD,
COOKING, KITCHEN TOOLS AND APPLIANCES!

WILMA ESPAILLAT ENGLISH
AND TOM ENGLISH

"[Tom and Wilma] ask readers to redefine hospitality by considering it from a biblical sense in this impassioned book."

—*Publishers Weekly*

THE HEART OF AN ANGEL
BECOMING GOD'S MESSENGERS OF LOVE
AND HOSPITALITY TO A WORLD IN NEED!

What does God *really* want?

Where does hospitality fit into the big picture?

Here's a complete, balanced, and Biblically-sound look at the practice of hospitality.

To help perform His divine will, God has frequently relied on a celebrated company of Heavenly messengers called angels. But in a manner of speaking, we're all called to be God's "Heavenly messengers" here on earth: we all have a story to tell, an experience to relate, a testimony to share; and, like His celestial band of servants, the Creator of the Universe wants each of us to become a Godly emissary of His supernatural love: following in the footsteps of Jesus Christ, through a lifestyle of giving, serving, encouraging, and ... sharing the Words of Life! But something's been holding us back from fully answering the call! We've lost an important truth that expresses the heart and nature of God, and we've abandoned a practice that's vital to peace and unity within our homes and communities, as well as the growth of our churches. It's one of the most misunderstood and neglected Biblical concepts today, and its inexcusable neglect is keeping us from becoming all God intended! God wants us to develop the "heart of an angel"—but how do we accomplish this? Better still, what is the heart of an angel? Join us as we examine the secrets of the heart: learn how to change the world while building meaningful relationships; strengthen your family while becoming more like God; unite your community while impacting eternity; and fulfill the Lord's greatest commandment while "flying" with the angels!

Do you have what it takes to join His band of "angels"?

God wants YOU!

"Bringing together all the Bible has to say about being hospitable, [this] forceful book will appeal to Christians interested in deeply scriptural reading."

—*BookLife (a division of Publishers Weekly)*

THE **HEART** OF AN **ANGEL!**

Becoming God's Messengers of Love and Hospitality to a World in Need!

TOM ENGLISH

WILMA ESPAILLAT ENGLISH

A Ravens' Read!

ISBN 978-0996693615 • Softcover • 192 pages

SPIRITUAL BOOT CAMP FOR CREATORS & DREAMERS: ENCOURAGEMENT, INSPIRATION & BASIC TRAINING TO HELP YOU ACHIEVE YOUR DREAMS

Are you a creative person? Do you have grand goals and high hopes? Are you chasing a seemingly impossible dream? More importantly, do you have what it takes? To fight fear, failure, and rejection? To weather the storms of life, defeat disappointment, and seize the day? To overcome all of the obstacles on the road to your destiny? To stay the course, no matter how tough it gets, or how long the journey takes?

Here you'll receive basic training specifically designed to whip you into shape so you can conquer your dreams and enjoy a victorious life. Tom and Wilma English share their personal battle tactics learned from decades in the trenches—practical strategies reinforced with truths from the Word of God—to encourage and help you to live each day in victory as you continue on the journey to realizing your hopes and dreams!

ISBN 978-0996693691 • Softcover • 272 pages

"...The Englishes write with style, clarity, and gracefulness. They contextualize their advice with real-world examples, while they develop most of their arguments thoroughly, persuasively, and with scriptural back-up.

"Ultimately, while it may look superficially similar to other books in its genre, Spiritual Boot Camp for Creators & Dreamers is uniquely thorough, well-written, persuasive, and inspiring. ...There are chapters about visualizing goals, managing time, finding and maintaining motivation, learning to pray, and other well-covered advice areas. Fortunately, their treatment of these common topics is fresh, with engaging, often surprising examples, such as the 15-page exploration of the story of Captain America. Further, some of the Englishes' advice is original to the authors, such as the chapters suggesting that readers find 'a Barnabas.' Also unique: the Englishes' jokes and their welcome approach to reconciling faith and science."

—The Booklife Prize, 2019

spiritual BOOT CAMP *for* Creators & Dreamers

ENCOURAGEMENT, INSPIRATION & BASIC TRAINING TO HELP YOU ACHIEVE YOUR DREAMS

TOM ENGLISH
★ ★ ★ ★ & ★ ★ ★ ★
WILMA ESPAILLAT ENGLISH

A Ravens' Read!

DIET FOR DREAMERS:
INSPIRATION TO FEED YOUR DREAMS,
ENCOURAGEMENT TO FOSTER YOUR CREATIVITY!

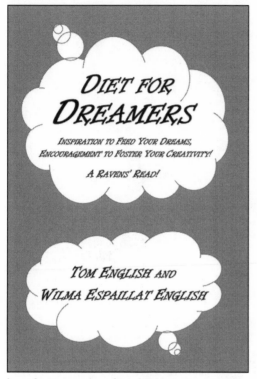

Got big dreams?
So, what do you feed them?

Everyone has a special dream. Whether you're an artist or a writer, an actor or a singer, an inventor or an entrepreneur; or just someone who dreams of better days ahead, Tom and Wilma want to help you achieve your goals, by encouraging you to faithfully pursue your dreams while providing you with practical advice and inspiring stories. In this collection you'll discover fascinating facts and a few humorous turns about men and women, young and old, who dreamed big and succeeded despite shaky circumstances, overwhelming obstacles and, often, the silly notions of our wonderful, whacky world.

Five dozen witty and inspiring articles highlighting everything from Sherlock Holmes to Slinky toys, Stan Lee to Lucille Ball, the Monkees to Mother's Day, Hershey's Chocolate to Julia Child, and much more. Plus, handling fear, rejection and failure.

ISBN 978-0979633577 • Softcover • 156 pages

Ravens' Reads:
Books to Feed Your Spirit!
AN IMPRINT OF **DEAD LETTER PRESS**

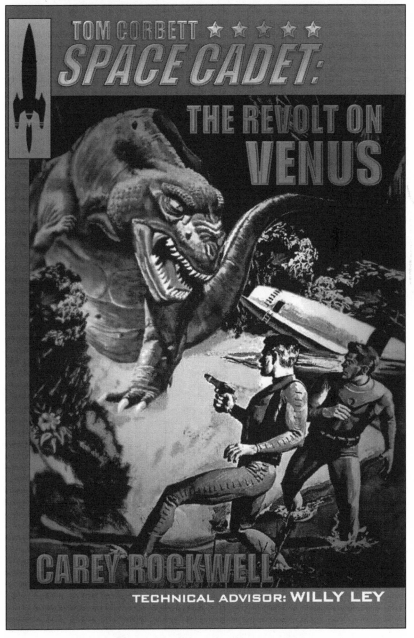

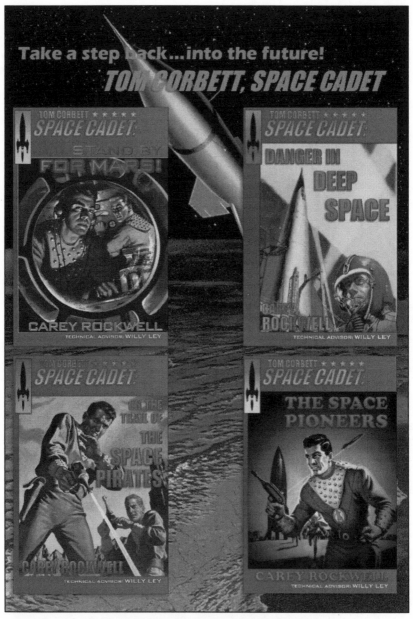

TOM CORBETT, SPACE CADET: STAND BY FOR MARS
(BOOK 1) ISBN 978-0996693622

TOM CORBETT, SPACE CADET: DANGER IN DEEP SPACE
(BOOK 2) ISBN 978-0996693639

TOM CORBETT, SPACE CADET: ON THE TRAIL OF THE SPACE PIRATES
(BOOK 3) ISBN 978-0996693646

TOM CORBETT, SPACE CADET: THE SPACE PIONEERS
(BOOK 4) ISBN 978-0996693653

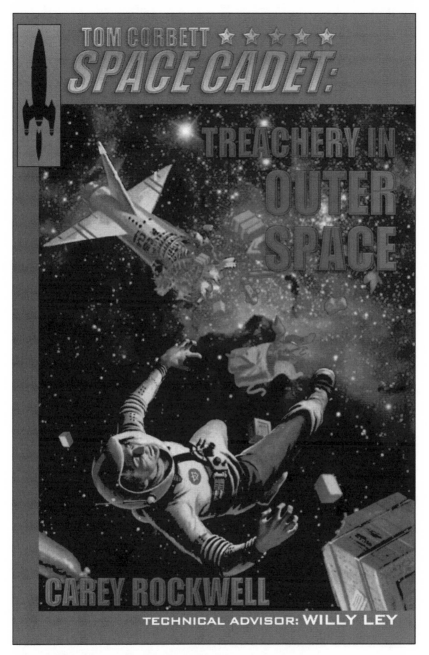

TOM CORBETT, SPACE CADET: TREACHERY IN OUTER SPACE
(BOOK 6) ISBN 978-1732434400

ALSO AVAILABLE:
TOM CORBETT, SPACE CADET: SABOTAGE IN SPACE
(BOOK 7) ISBN 978-1732434455

PLEASE DON'T MISS A SINGLE VOLUME OF BLACK INFINITY, THE RETRO-FLAVORED, ILLUSTRATED BOOK OF SCIENCE FICTION ADVENTURE STORIES & SPECIAL FEATURES

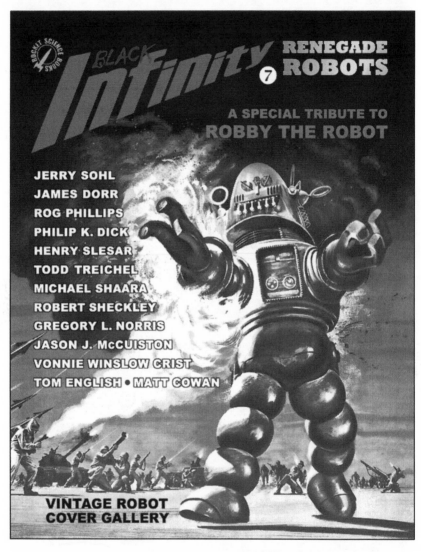

Black Infinity ⑨ **FIRST CONTACT**

GEORGE PAL'S
THE WAR OF THE WORLDS

THE ORIGINAL
BATTLESTAR GALACTICA

RAY BRADBURY
MURRAY LEINSTER
ROBERT SILVERBERG
VONNIE WINSLOW CRIST
JAMES DORR · JEROME BIXBY
LEIGH BRACKETT · DAMON KNIGHT
JUSTIN HUMPHREYS · DOUGLAS SMITH
GREGORY L. NORRIS · JASON J. McCUISTON

EDITED BY TOM ENGLISH
AVAILABLE AT AMAZON, BN.COM AND OTHER ONLINE
VENUES, OR ORDER THROUGH YOUR LOCAL BOOKSTORE